SPORTS SPONSORSHIP

Getting your share

By Brian Sims

D1434891

Bro.

This bo

5th Floor, Mermaid House, 2 Puddle Dock, London EC4V 3DS
Tel: 44 (0) 20 7332 2000 • Fax: 44 (0) 20 7332 2003 • ISDN: 44 (0) 20 7236 2530
E-mail: info@hazletonpublishing.com • Website: www.hazletonpublishing.com

Hazleton Publishing

Foreword

We cannot switch on our TVs, PCs, watch live sport or even see a film, without being aware of sponsorship. At the heart of sponsors' efforts is the desire for the public to buy more of their products or services through brand building, either directly or indirectly.

Sponsorship itself is merely a vehicle to this end. Within business, its cost has to be balanced against other opportunities to increase sales. These can include straight advertising, recruiting more salespeople, refreshing old product ranges and introducing bonus schemes for existing staff and so on.

The equation that runs through a sponsor's mind is: 'If we spend £x, will we be likely get twice as much in return?' It comes down to basic maths and includes the same uncertainties as most other investment opportunities.

The mistake most often made by those seeking sponsorship is not looking on it as a mathematical equation from the perspective of the sponsor. They don't do the maths to a sufficient level of detail.

To a sponsor there is a world of difference between the following proposals:
1. "If you give me some money, you can put your stickers on my car, which goes really fast and I'm bound to win. Some people will see it, and that'll be great!"
2. "If you give me £500, approximately 10,000 people will be exposed to your logos for a period of 30 minutes. This means that you will have bought 5,000 man hours of exposure to your target socio-economic group. Your existing experience is that 500 man-hours of exposure generates one new client. Your average client profitability value is £100. This means that you might reasonably expect to gain ten new clients, providing £1,000 of profitability, for your £500 marketing spend. You therefore only need to gain five new clients to break even.'

Now the second example is a little simplistic and not always easy to calculate. However, it is far more persuasive than the all too commonly experienced approach shown in the first example.

Increasing technology has resulted in spiralling costs in many sports. What constantly surprises me is that the sophistication of sport's attempts to attract the funding necessary to succeed hasn't kept equal pace with their sporting efforts.

This book is highly practical and provides a clear understanding of sponsors' perspectives, together with some simple tools and disciplines. It becomes increasingly apparent that such a publication is desperately needed by the industry. I'm glad that you have just purchased, or are about to purchase a copy. It will help to make all our business lives a little easier.

John Reed
Chief Executive
Arbuthnot Latham

John Reed is the Chief Executive Officer of Arbuthnot Latham & Co Limited, a private bank offering banking and wealth management services to private clients. Together with lawyer Edward Lock of Lock & Marlborough and Phil Harris of Harris & Co chartered accountants and several other industry figures, they have founded the Arbuthnot Latham Motorsport Partnership to help develop the careers of young aspiring racing drivers.

Contents

Introduction

Sports sponsorship is not a right. Nor is it a charity. It has to be earned. After listening to some sports competitors talking to the media, you could be forgiven for thinking just the opposite. According to many of them, the fact that they want to be professional competitors is reason enough to expect a company to support them financially. With this attitude, is it any wonder that sponsorship gets a bad name and becomes increasingly difficult to obtain?

I want to make it clear what this book is about. It has been written specifically for those of you who want to obtain sports sponsorship. As such, it is a book about selling. I don't profess to be an expert on all aspects of sports sponsorship, but I can claim to have been successful in obtaining a high level of it.

The book is based very much on my own experiences in securing sponsorship within international motor racing, over a period of some 30 years. Many of these deals were for my own driving career, whilst others have been for teams up to and including Formula 1. The techniques that I've outlined are not simply theoretical. I know that they can work, because I've used nearly all of them myself.

It's true to say that in motorsport, perhaps more than with any other sport, the need for sponsorship starts at a very early age. Without a kart, racing or rally car, how else are you going to compete? The cost of buying or even hiring these, let alone running them competitively, is beyond the reach of most people. The need to learn, at an early age, how to obtain sponsorship is therefore extremely important to anyone wanting to compete at any level of the sport.

Although many of the examples in the book come from motorsport, I would like to think that they could help sponsorship-seekers across a wide range of sports. Whether you are an individual competitor or have been given the task of securing sponsorship for your local football team, the principles are very similar. Perhaps you are embarking on a career in sports marketing with an agency, or already work for a sports association that requires sponsorship for one of its championships. The skills that you need are very much the same.

I am still learning this business after 30 years. I hope that by passing some of my experiences on to you – both successful and unsuccessful – it will help you to not only find that much needed sponsorship, but also to understand the importance of looking after the sponsor, so that you develop a mutually beneficial long-term relationship.

Brian Sims

Confidence in your own ability

I doubt if there is another word in the English language that has seen a greater increase in usage over the last three decades than "sponsorship". Even five-year-olds now understand what it means, thanks to their teachers encouraging them to find sponsors for various fund-raising activities at their schools.

It's not only in sport that commercial sponsorship has become commonplace. Sponsorship is equally popular in education, the arts, charities, fashion, broadcasting, music and conservation – to name just a few areas.

It is sport, however, that most people immediately think of when they talk about sponsorship. Think Formula 1, the Premiership, the Olympics, the Champions League, The Grand National and the Rugby World Cup, and you can't help but associate them with high profile corporate sponsors. Can you imagine a Formula 1 car that isn't emblazoned with brand names? It would look totally out of place on the grid. But it wasn't always like that.

When I first started watching motor racing in Britain, back in the mid-'60s, the only names that you saw on racing cars were those of trade suppliers, such as Dunlop, Castrol, BP and Shell. Grand Prix cars were usually painted in the national colours of the manufacturer. Red for Italy, British racing green and the blue of France. Today, only Ferrari – now that Jaguar's Formula 1 experiment has collapsed – still stick to that principle.

Commercial advertising was also taboo in most other sports at that time. Football shirts simply carried the club's badge, whilst the mere prospect of commercial branding on the side of a yacht would have sent many a sailing club Commodore into an apoplectic fit.

In 1968, however, just about everyone in sport took notice when Colin Chapman, the legendary boss of the Lotus Formula 1 Grand Prix Team, took advantage of a change in the rules that governed motorsport in Europe and negotiated a lucrative sponsorship deal with tobacco giants John Player & Sons.

That year, Chapman entered his two drivers, Jim Clark and Graham Hill, in the 1968 Formula 1 World Championship. Their cars were painted to look like cigarette packets on four wheels. The Team was called Gold Leaf Team Lotus, promoting the Player's brand of the same name. Since that momentous deal, the tobacco industry has been the primary sponsor of the majority of Formula 1 teams, pumping in hundreds of millions of pounds in return for high profile branding on the cars, drivers and just about everything else that can be seen at a Grand Prix race weekend.

It's all about to change, of course, and tobacco sponsorship in Formula 1 will disappear in the same way that it already has in most other sports. Nevertheless, its impact and positive effect on attitudes to sponsorship across virtually all sports should never be under-estimated.

Sponsorship has now effectively become the lifeblood of the majority of sports – but don't think that it's only at a professional level that this happens. I'm sure that those of you who have children involved in sport, even at a very junior level, will know only too well about the ever increasing costs of equipment, training, or even travel to and from events. The only option for many parents is to seek help via a company's marketing budget. In other words, they need to find sponsorship.

Here in the UK, the sponsorship industry is now worth an estimated £500 million per year and is still growing. It's only when you look at the high number of sports that are seeking their share of that sponsorship cake, that you realise the incredible competitiveness of the situation.

It wasn't long ago that sponsorship used to be regarded as the poor cousin of advertising. That situation has changed dramatically and specialist sponsorship agencies and consultancies have sprung up all over the world. Just about every aspect of sponsorship management, commercial exploitation and implementation is now on offer. Some of these agencies have become major global corporations. One of the most famous is IMG, started by the late Mark McCormack. IMG

"Less than 10 per cent of all sponsorship-related agencies and consultancies are able to offer assistance in terms of finding sponsors"

specialises in the management of international sports stars and the promotion of international sports events to which, more often than not, they own the commercial rights.

Many other agencies offer a range of niche skills. Some work with companies to help them extract a viable commercial return from their sponsorship investment, whilst others provide a service for measuring the impact of sports sponsorship expenditure. In the process, they will analyse every aspect of TV viewing statistics and print-media exposure. This provides sponsors, sports teams and associations with essential information for measuring how well sponsorship programmes are performing.

That's great, I'm sure you are saying to yourself, if you're a sponsor or if you have a sponsor who needs assistance and expertise in making the sponsorship work. But what about the task of finding sponsors in the first place? Where does the help come from to do that? Unfortunately, this is where matters become a little more difficult.

I would estimate that less than 10 per cent of all sponsorship-related agencies and consultancies are able to offer assistance in terms of finding sponsors. In other words, these businesses do not employ sales personnel. At best, if you approach them with a sponsorship opportunity, they will present it to the companies that they already represent. If those companies aren't interested, that's usually as far as it will go.

So why is it difficult to find agencies or consultants that are interested in selling sponsorship opportunities on your behalf? The answer is surprisingly straightforward. Selling sponsorship is considered by most sports marketing agencies to be extremely difficult and very risky, particularly when a meaningful regular income can more easily be earned managing a client's sponsorship portfolio or consulting on behalf of a sports association or team. The income that can be generated from the commission on a sponsorship deal might be extremely lucrative, in some cases up to 20 per cent of the sponsorship fee obtained, but there are no guarantees that the deals will be done.

The days of tobacco advertising in European motorsport are numbered

Not only that, but there is often a long time gap between an agency concluding a deal and the commission being paid to them. This is due to the commission only being paid when money is received by the sponsored party. In addition, it's not unusual for there to be a high level of expenditure incurred throughout the sales process. This is particularly true in the event of international sponsorship deals, where sales personnel's travelling expenses and international phone calls can quickly build up, in addition to all the costs incurred in creating and producing a professional standard presentation and other sales material.

The majority of those agencies or consultancies which are prepared to look for sponsors on behalf of an individual, team or organisation, will almost certainly insist on a monthly retainer being paid, irrespective of success and will usually expect all their expenses to be covered. In addition they will take a commission on any sponsorship that they secure. There are many people who object to paying a retainer, but I don't see why they should. It's a notoriously tough market to be in and to expect a salesperson with a track record in delivering sponsorship to work on a commission-only basis is rather unrealistic. Why should the salesperson carry all of the risk?

I have to say that a large number of motorsport teams and drivers do expect something for nothing in this respect. They are not prepared to go out and find their own sponsorship, but they continually moan that businesses aren't supporting them. Ask drivers to find £1,000 for a new helmet that supposedly gives them an aerodynamic advantage and they'll somehow find the money, even though there is no guarantee that it will actually improve their performance. Some of them will find the money to acquire a luxurious motorhome to spend time in at the track. However, if you ask them to pay a reasonable retainer to a specialist with a proven track record in securing sponsorship, the very lifeblood of all their activities, they will come up with every reason in the book as to why they shouldn't do this. Of course, it's a very short-sighted practice. In my experience, it is the teams and drivers who are either willing to put in the effort themselves, or who are prepared to invest in securing the services of a professional sponsorship sales consultant or agency, that will ultimately secure long-term, meaningful sponsorships.

Sponsorship DIY

The employment of a professional agency or consultant is fine if you are able to afford it, but what if you can't? What if you are an individual sports competitor, a team or a sports association that just doesn't have that type of budget available? What if you don't have an in-house marketing team to work on your behalf?

There's a simple answer. Do it yourself. Although sponsorship-seeking is not easy, it is not beyond the capability of anyone who is prepared to go about it in a logical manner and who is prepared to put in a great deal of effort. I should stress that you must also be able to cope with rejection, because for every "yes" that you get, there will be a multitude of "no's". If you can't take this, you really should think very carefully before getting involved in this business.

It might surprise some of you to hear that the principles which form the basis of sponsorship-seeking are very similar, whatever the level of sponsorship that you require. I've tried to make this book as applicable to the parents of a youngster who are perhaps seeking sponsorship worth a few hundred pounds to enable their child to take part in a junior championship event, as it will be to the marketing manager of a sports stadium who is seeking significant sponsorship for a new event.

It's my belief that if you are prepared to take the time to work your way through this book and are willing to put into practice some of the ideas and suggestions that you'll come across, there is no reason why any of you shouldn't be successful in securing meaningful sports sponsorship.

I must warn you, however, not to expect me to divulge some magic formula, which will guarantee your success. If there is one, I certainly haven't found it! What I have found is a systematic approach to obtaining sponsorship that has worked well for me over many years. There is no reason why it shouldn't help you to be successful, provided that you are willing to accept that there is no substitute in this business for hard work. I can't even guarantee that you will get out what you put in. What I do know, however, is that if you're not prepared to constantly learn new ideas and to put in a huge amount of effort, you have little chance of being successful.

SUMMARY

Sponsorship is the lifeblood of many sports. At all levels of sport there is an increasing demand for sponsorship. Very few worthwhile agencies or sponsorship consultants will work on your behalf to find sponsorship for you, without a sizeable financial retainer being paid.

The skills needed to successfully obtain sponsorship can be learned. We can all sell. It's simply a case of enhancing the style that you feel most comfortable using.

It will involve a lot of hard work and more than a little heartache. But there is no reason why you shouldn't become a competent exponent of sponsorship acquisition, if you understand the basic reasons why companies use sponsorship as a marketing tool.

A **professional** approach

I f you are going to be successful in securing meaningful sponsorship in a highly competitive market, you've either got to be incredibly lucky or else you need to develop some effective professional selling skills. Calm down! That doesn't mean you have to become a foot-in-the-door salesperson. What it means is that you will first of all need to understand just what constitutes a saleable sponsorship opportunity, then you will need to develop an effective way of presenting this to potential sponsors.

Looking at my own background, I consider myself fortunate that before I moved into professional sport, I'd enjoyed a successful career in the corporate world. This included working for Rank Xerox, a company whose own internal sales-training programmes were so highly regarded at the time that they launched a company which marketed them to other businesses. I think I learned more about selling in my time at Xerox than in any other company for whom I worked.

After Xerox, I went on to become the UK Sales Training Director for the global ITT Corporation, who at that time owned many high profile companies, such as Koni Shock Absorbers, Rimmel Cosmetics, Sheraton Hotels and Avis Car Rentals.

I derived a great deal of satisfaction from training people in the skills necessary to present business opportunities in a professional and effective manner. I always worked on the basis that everyone has their own style of inter-personal communication. The key is to help them understand the ways in which that style can be most effectively used. It is not to try to mould them into clones, all quoting the same spiel.

When I first started looking into ways of finding sponsorship for my own racing, there was very little help available. I remember trying to buy books on the subject without any success, until I eventually discovered Mark McCormack's excellent book, What They Don't Teach You At Harvard Business School. I still have that book, which I am proud to say the great man personally signed when he hosted a seminar that I attended in South Africa. It's a worthwhile read and I learned a great deal from it.

To this day, rather surprisingly, the amount of material available to help potential sponsorship seekers is extremely limited, which is one of the reasons why I designed and ran a training course on the subject at the Williams F1 Conference Centre in 2003. Having received some welcome feedback from those who attended the course, it seemed a logical progression to write this book.

It is often said that salespeople are born, not made. I don't subscribe to that at all. It makes no more sense than saying that car drivers are born, not made. I accept that some people are more naturally gifted than others in their driving capabilities, but there are very few people who can't be taught to become competent behind the wheel. The same applies to selling sponsorship opportunities. How successful a person ultimately becomes will have a great deal to do with other qualities. As in sport, your levels of dedication, focus, perseverance and hard work will play a major role in determining your ultimate success.

I can already hear some of you saying that you're not the type to be a salesperson and that you've never really been able to sell. Please don't put this book down just yet! I want you to forget for a

"Your level of confidence will grow considerably once you discover that you can genuinely provide a solution to his or her needs"

minute about the business world. I want you to think about your own private life. We're all salespeople, like it or not. Have you ever asked a person to go on a date? Have you ever asked your bank manager for a loan? Have you been successful at a job interview? Have you ever talked your spouse or partner into going to a holiday resort that they weren't keen on visiting? If the answer to any of these questions is "yes" then please don't tell me that you can't sell. You can! Most people are selling themselves all the time; to friends, relatives, boyfriends, girlfriends, potential employers and even to prospective husbands and wives. What you really mean is that you don't feel confident about doing it on a business basis, particularly with strangers and especially in an unfriendly environment. That I can understand. There are several reasons for this lack of confidence, but with most people, the main ones are:
• Fear of rejection
• Fear of the unknown
• Fear of failure.

These same fears prevent a lot of people from succeeding at a variety of activities. Don't worry about admitting that they apply to you. They apply to about 95 per cent of the population and it's only if they don't apply to you that you should start worrying. Even top sports performers will tell you that if they don't get really nervous before the start of their particular competitive event, they rarely perform well. I've known several who were so scared that they were sometimes physically sick. James Hunt, the late Formula 1 World Champion, was one.

The difference is that they have learned to overcome these fears and use their nervousness in a beneficial and positive way, giving them an extra edge to their performance. What they will also tell you is that their nervousness and fear of failure is balanced by the confidence that comes from knowing that they have prepared as well as is possible.

This is no difference in selling. If you have the confidence that comes from knowing you have prepared in a professional manner and followed a clearly planned strategy, just as the athlete has a strictly adhered-to training schedule, then you will have gone a long way to reducing your fears. For a start, you will know what to expect when you make contact with your potential sponsor. Your level of confidence will grow considerably once you discover that you can genuinely provide a solution to his or her needs. This book is all about finding the most effective ways of doing just that.

Anglian Windows was another successful Formula Ford sponsorship deal that Brian negotiated for his own racing career. The car is pictured on the grid at Thruxton

"You won't get far if you try to hard-sell the opportunity and don't listen to the potential buyer"

Think about your own buying habits. When you go out to buy a TV, a sound system or perhaps even a car, take a careful note of how the salesperson acts. Do they give you confidence that they know what they're talking about, or do you buy despite them? What is it that makes you feel that you are buying from them, rather than being sold to? What perhaps causes you to resent buying from a particular salesperson? Do they generate your respect as being professional? You can learn a great deal by observing how people try to sell to you and noting what works and what doesn't.

It's a fact that in this highly competitive world, more and more people are developing a resistance to being sold to. We are constantly being bombarded by sales campaigns. Nothing is more irritating than being interrupted in the middle of your evening meal by a telesales person, whatever the product or service that they are offering. You advertise in Auto Trader and immediately get half a dozen calls from competitive magazines trying to switch you to their publication. In the same way, a lot of people dislike being approached at a motorway service centre by a salesperson trying to hoist yet another credit card onto them. As if they haven't got enough!

Perhaps the words "selling" and "salesperson" are the real problem. To many people, the words conjure up an image of a smooth, fast-talking, forceful, persistent individual of the type you associate with second-hand car lots. The major skill attributed to them is the "gift of the gab" and there are still plenty of those around. The problem is that if you want to be successful at securing commercial sponsorship, those traits won't get you very far at all.

Before you think that I'm maligning salespeople, let me dispel that idea. I have always been proud to call myself a salesman, whatever my official title may have been. I also happen to believe that while the skills needed to be a professional salesperson might have changed, the need for high quality, professional salespeople hasn't. Imagine a world without salespeople. You are thinking about buying a digital camera for the first time. Of course you can go on-line and read all of the information about the products available, but that doesn't always answer all of your questions. Don't you feel more comfortable if, before making a decision, you can talk face-to-face with someone who really knows the products inside out, and who can answer questions that actually relate to you and your needs? No, you don't like being sold to, but you do want to learn as much as you can about the best choice for your particular circumstances. Surely what you want is for that salesperson to determine exactly what you want the camera to be capable of and also your budgetary constraints, then demonstrate to you which models will best suit your requirements. Done professionally, isn't that better than simply choosing from a brochure? It's still selling, but selling in a way that most people find acceptable.

Don't try to hard-sell sponsorship

What really brasses people off is the salesperson who doesn't listen to what you want, and who is more interested in his need to sell the product than in finding the one most suitable for your needs. Instead of listening to what you are saying, he is busting a gut to get on with what he wants to say.

Marketing a sponsorship opportunity is no different. You won't get far if you try to hard-sell the opportunity and don't listen to the prospect (the potential buyer). You need to identify a company's marketing objectives and then demonstrate that your sponsorship opportunity can help that company achieve some of those objectives in a cost-effective manner. No more or no less than just that. If your opportunity isn't right for them, that's not a problem. You simply ask them if they can introduce you to any business contacts for whom it might be appropriate and then leave, creating in the process a professional image, so that you can always go back if another opportunity presents itself that better suits their requirements.

So, relax. It's not my intention to turn you into a Del Boy!

Over the years I have been very fortunate in negotiating many sponsorship deals, but I have to admit to being unsuccessful on far more occasions. Very often, what I had to offer simply didn't match the company's needs at the time. That's very much the name of the game. You have to recognise this and not let it get you down. Hopefully, though, by taking on board the information in this book, you'll be able to improve your own personal performance level and learn something useful from my own experiences, both successful and unsuccessful.

SUMMARY

You sell every day of your life. It is not correct to say that salespeople are born, not made. People dislike selling because they fear rejection, the unknown and failure.

Increasingly, everyone is developing a resistance to intrusive salespeople. Fortunately, the old "foot in the door" style has had its day. People want to buy, as opposed to being sold to.

Professional sponsorship selling requires a high level of integrity and a genuine belief that you will only recommend your sponsorship if you know that it is capable of helping the company achieve its stated objectives.

No need to be a **champion**

The very first time I watched a motor race was at Brands Hatch in Kent, on a freezing cold Boxing Day, far too long ago to remember the exact year. I had been invited by some friends, and I recall standing on a frozen grass bank, thinking to myself what heroes these drivers were. Tyres screaming, cars spinning, the crowd cheering and stacks of adrenalin in the air. Yes, I thought, I could really get to like this.

In those days, it wasn't as easy as it is today to experience the thrills of driving on a racetrack. Red Letter Driving Experience Days hadn't been invented and racing schools were few and far between. Nevertheless, a few years after that first taste of motor racing, I managed to get the cash together to pay for a trial lesson at the Brands Hatch racing driver school, which was appropriately called Motor Racing Stables. I remember being taken round the circuit by one-time Grand Prix driver Pete Arundel in a TVR Vixen, before eventually being let loose behind the wheel myself for a couple of laps in a Formula Ford. This was a single-seater racing car, like a smaller version of a Formula 1 car. It was an experience that was beyond my wildest dreams – although I didn't exactly cover myself in glory when I spun the car.

That was all it took. I was definitely going to become a racing driver! Of course, at that age you don't ask yourself silly questions such as where the money was going to come from to both buy and maintain a racing car. So for the next couple of years I had to be content with making my road cars look and sound as competitive as money would allow. I shudder with embarrassment at the thought of that now.

It was in 1972 that I finally decided to go for broke and enrol at the famous Jim Russell Racing Driver School, then based at Snetterton, in Norfolk. My instructor, John Kirkpatrick, had just started at the School. He eventually went on to own the business and became a good friend. Some 16 years later, John came out to my own racing driver school in South Africa to be a judge in our annual competition, the Camel Rookie of the Year Challenge, which I had created to identify our top pupil.

While attending my first course at the Jim Russell School, I used to stay at a small hotel in the vicinity of Snetterton, called Bunwell Manor. It was owned by another of the school's instructors, and I spent many a happy evening over supper discussing with him and a few other wannabe Formula 1 stars, the technicalities of race car driving. I remember thinking that there was nothing that I wanted more than to become a professional racing driver.

The problem existed even in those days, that unless you had a fair amount of money, it was difficult to get started in racing. At that time, I was working as a salesman for the Goodyear Tyre Company, selling earthmover and truck tyres. Despite winning the Goodyear Sword of Honour as the company's top UK salesman, I still wasn't earning anywhere near enough money to contemplate buying my own race car. A sword doesn't make up for a lack of money.

A chance meeting with a woman at a party was to help change that situation. She told me that she worked for the photocopier manufacturer, Rank Xerox, and that the company was looking for new sales people. At first I wasn't interested in the idea of selling photocopiers for a living.

"Can you imagine what would happen if we put that car, emblazoned with your branding, in the middle of a shopping centre on a Saturday morning?"

Then she told me how much commission their sales personnel were earning. It was nearly three times more than I was getting at Goodyear and so I went along for an interview and was lucky enough to become a Xerox salesman. Little did I realise at the time, that this decision would eventually help me build a career in Formula 1.

Financing my passion

My Xerox employment started with a three-week course at the company's residential sales-training school. In those days, even the Rank Xerox secretaries, engineers and customer relation officers were sent on sales training courses, such was the philosophy within Xerox that everyone who came into contact with the outside world was effectively a salesperson and should be trained properly.

Xerox was a great company to work for. At that time they had over 1,000 UK salespeople and each year we all attended a sales conference in London. One year in particular sticks in my memory: After the sales conference, we all went to the Grosvenor Hotel in Park Lane for the official dinner. The entertainment was provided by a (surprisingly flat) Ronnie Corbett, whom I recall was booed off the stage and pelted with bread rolls by some of the more vociferous of the sales team. He was followed on stage by Pan's People, who were then Top of the Pops' regular dance group and, back then, could best be described as real stunners. They were still quite naïve, however, because they had to run for their lives after being foolish enough to ask if a few of the 1,000 sales staff, of whom about 85 per cent were male, would like to come up and dance with them on-stage!

For me, the highlight of the evening was the traditional speech by the chairman, in which he ecstatically praised the sales force for delivering the company's best ever results. At the end of this rousing oration, it was common practice for him to allow a few questions from the floor. One brave salesman stood up.

"If we are such a superb sales team and have made the company so much money," he said, "I would like to know why we have to drive 1100cc two-door Ford Escorts as our company cars?"

Quick as a flash, the Chairman replied: "Because I haven't yet finalised the deal with Ford to build one-door Ford Escorts!"

Within two years of joining Xerox, I'd saved enough to buy a racing car. It was a modified Ford Escort and I bought it from Nick Whiting, one of the three Whiting brothers. Charlie Whiting went on to become Formula 1's Technical Director. Poor Nick, himself a talented racing driver, perished in an unsolved murder case. I dabbled with this car for a couple of races before realising that I really wanted to drive a single-seater racing car, similar to the one that I had driven at my

Brands Hatch: where a passion was born – and a career made
Insert: the launch of Brian Sims' first ever sponsorship deal, Victoria's Night Club, in 1974

very first session at Brands Hatch. In the 70s, Formula Ford 1600 offered by far the best opportunity for an aspiring young driver and I traded in my saloon car for a secondhand Crossle Formula Ford complete with a trailer. The problem was, I now had a car but didn't have the budget to run it competitively.

What I needed was a sponsor, but I had already convinced myself that this was impossible, as I hadn't built up any sort of track record in racing. Then, one day, I really took myself to task: Brian you are a salesman, you've sold a lot of photocopiers for Xerox and you've had some superb sales training. If you want to race professionally, get out there and find a sponsor! For once, I spoke some sense. It took me just over a month to achieve my goal.

I realised that due to work commitments, I would only have the time that year to race at my local track, Brands Hatch. I decided therefore, that it would be appropriate to approach companies in that specific area. I tried about half a dozen, with absolutely no interest. Then one day, on a business trip to Ashford, I was driving along the old A20 when I passed what looked like a building site. A large sign caught my eye:

"New nightclub opening on March 1"

I drove on to my meeting, storing that information in my mind. Over the weekend I did a little research. Remember, this was in the days before the introduction of mobile phones and the

Internet, so research was a lot more difficult then than it is for sponsorship-seekers today. What I found out was interesting. The new club was to be called Victoria's and it would target 21-45 year olds as members, providing them with a luxurious restaurant, dance floor and a bar. Membership wasn't too expensive, putting it within the range of a wide variety of people. I recall sitting down in a Happy Eater with a note pad, writing down what I thought would be Victoria's likely marketing needs, with a view to attracting new membership. I then developed my strategy.

A week later, I towed my Formula Ford on its trailer to Victoria's car park and positioned it prominently across the front entrance to the club. As I had hoped, there were quite a few people already arriving for lunch. I'd previously checked to see if the owner was likely to be there that day and so I walked in and asked if I could talk to him about an idea for creating awareness of his nightclub. When he eventually came through to the front reception area, I simply asked him to look out of the window into the car park area.

As I had anticipated, a group of people had by now gathered around the racing car, having a good nosey at it, as often happens when you pull up in a crowded place. I waited for a couple of seconds, before posing the question: "Can you imagine what would happen if we put that car, emblazoned with Victoria's branding, in the middle of Maidstone shopping centre on a Saturday morning?" That was all it took to achieve my objective – a meeting with him to look at ways in which my racing programme could help him sell more membership, help develop a potential customer database, introduce the motor racing fraternity to his club and create awareness of it through the local media.

The outcome was that I went on to successfully negotiate my very first sponsorship deal. With some of the budget that was agreed, I had the car and my helmet painted in the aubergine and gold livery of Victoria's and had hundreds of car stickers printed.

I also generated a fair amount of media coverage for his business by organising a press launch at Victoria's to announce the sponsorship.

Early success

That season I was able to introduce a lot of new members to the club, each providing me with commission as part of the sponsorship deal. More importantly, I had learned a very important lesson. Not once during the negotiations did the owner of Victoria's ever ask me how good I was as a race driver, how quick the car was, or what my ambitions in racing were. He was only interested in finding out what the use of a racing car as a marketing tool could do for his business.

I see many sponsorship proposals based almost entirely on the level of success achieved in a particular sport by the presenter. Whilst performance standards can often play a major role in the decision-making process, it normally only happens when a high profile club or individual is involved, or when a company will be basing its marketing strategy specifically on a competitor's performance, as in the case of a sports shoe manufacturer, for example. For the majority of sponsorship-seekers it is, at best, only a minor consideration and is usually looked at only in the final stages of a negotiation. The harsh reality is that most sponsorship decisions are based on the benefit to a company's bottom line, not on how good the competitor is.

SUMMARY

You don't have to be a winning competitor or team to obtain sponsorship. Your level of performance is less important than the potential for a business return that your sponsorship opportunity offers. You need to be creative and bold if you are going to interest companies in looking at your sponsorship opportunity.

Chapter

4

Why do companies **sponsor?**

It shouldn't need rocket science to realise that for a sponsorship proposal to be of interest it has to meet at least some of the real, not the assumed, marketing needs of a company. So why is it that when I talk at length to corporate marketing people about the high number of sponsorship proposals they receive, I still find that most of them will agree on one point? They all tell me that a very high number of the proposals which they receive display a total lack of understanding of what their company is likely to want within a sponsorship programme.

This is such a fundamental and critical part of the sponsorship sales process that unless you have a proper understanding of it, everything else that is covered in this book will be a waste of time. If you don't appreciate the range of reasons why a company considers sponsorship to be a valuable part of its marketing mix, you'll find it incredibly difficult, if not impossible, to demonstrate how your sponsorship opportunity can deliver any worthwhile benefits.

I think it's fair to say that if you were to conduct a survey among sponsorship seekers, asking if they can list the main reasons why companies sponsor, the majority of people would list the two main reasons as brand awareness and hospitality.

Without doubt, these are two very important criteria for many sponsors. However, if you rely only on these two factors, you'll struggle to interest many companies. Imagine going to a restaurant and finding that there are only two choices on the menu. What if you don't really fancy either of them? What will you do? Go somewhere else, of course. It's the same with only offering brand awareness and hospitality to a potential sponsor. If neither of these two major entitlements really turn a company on, it won't spend a great deal of time trying to find out what else you could offer. It will simply go somewhere else – to a person or organisation that is offering a sponsorship opportunity capable of meeting their needs.

The list of reasons why companies become a commercial sponsor is almost endless. To simplify the task I want to identify the factors that in my experience are the most common. I should stress that these aren't in any order of importance and also that this is a far from complete list. I've usually found that it is a combination of many of these factors that result in a sponsorship agreement being reached.

Brand awareness

There is no doubt that brand awareness is extremely important to certain companies in deciding whether or not to use sponsorship as a marketing tool. Undoubtedly the most blatant business sector in recent years to use sponsorship as a way of increasing brand awareness has been the tobacco industry, which has paid premium prices to be seen on televised sporting events, including Formula 1, snooker, motorcycle racing and yachting. There are many other business sectors that seek high levels of brand awareness, such as mobile phones, IT, soft drinks and clothing. But there are many types of business to whom it is less important. A management consultancy, for example, or a company that sells expensive industrial cutting equipment would typically not see the need to spend huge sums of money promoting its name to a wide audience. The public at large are not going to be its target market, so why spend money promoting the company name in that way? But there are many other ways in which these companies can effectively benefit from the use of sports sponsorship. Such as these:

Corporate hospitality

The same companies that I have just identified as being uninterested in brand awareness may well see the importance of certain types of hospitality in a sponsorship proposal. The opportunity to invite clients, or prospective clients, to join their management team at a sporting event can be very effective for a company. In Formula 1, for example, on the Sunday of a Grand Prix, the VIP Paddock Club is full of company directors, many of them involved as sponsors. Many others are prospective or existing clients who have been invited by sponsors. The opportunity to spend seven or eight hours together without the interruption of phones and other office distractions can be highly rewarding from a business perspective. This can apply just as effectively with various levels of hospitality. It doesn't have to be at the level in which Formula 1 operates for the concept to work well for a company.

It's important to bear in mind, however, that it is very easy to fall into a trap. Sports hospitality is a booming and highly competitive industry in its own right and companies are being approached all the time to buy hospitality at major sporting events. Favourite hospitality venues include Wimbledon, Twickenham and Ascot. Many sponsorship proposals that rely too heavily on the provision of corporate hospitality are rejected because a company decides that it can achieve the same objective by booking the corporate hospitality, without the added expense of a sponsorship involvement.

Image transfer

This is an important aspect of sponsorship that is commonly overlooked. Very often, companies will respond to a proposal that highlights the benefits of brand awareness by informing you that they can guarantee the same or an even higher level of awareness through conventional advertising. Why, they will ask, should they take the risk with sponsorship?

There is one very important factor that can be used to answer that objection. It's a prime reason why many companies become involved in sponsorship. It is known as Image Transfer. But what does it mean? I'll use Formula 1 as an example. Think for a minute of the various qualities or images that you might associate with the Formula 1 World Championship. I'm not saying that there aren't some negative emotions as well, but think of all the positive ones. Here are just a few that you might come up with: aspirational, global, hi-tech, glamorous, colourful, exciting, competitive, skilful, fast, team work, powerful, trendy, fashionable, dynamic, elite.

Now, put yourselves in the shoes of the marketing director of a company that you are approaching. There are many qualities with which he would like his company or brand to be associated. He considers it important to project these qualities to his target market. If he can be convinced that the qualities that Formula 1 projects match a high number of those that he is looking to promote, it creates a very powerful reason for him to consider sponsorship opportunities within Formula 1.

For example, if he wants his brand of male toiletries to be perceived as being expensive, macho and elite, Formula 1 might be a very good platform for him. The perceptions of Formula 1 can be shown to match those qualities. It could be argued that boxing, for example, would not provide such perceptions, although it has other qualities that might suit a different company. By being involved in Formula 1, his company could benefit from the "image transfer" that comes from people mentally linking the qualities of Grand Prix racing to his company's brand of male toiletries.

Conventional advertising might be able to create brand awareness for that company, but what it can't do as well as sponsorship is create the emotive response that comes from being associated with the qualities that we identified as being important. So if you can list all of the qualities that could be associated with your specific sport, you can build a very good case to put forward. When you talk to your prospect, ask him to list some of the qualities that he or she would equate with their brand. You can then draw examples from the list that you've mentally compiled and equate the two.

Public Relations

Public Relations is yet another important factor in looking at the reasons why companies sponsor. The trouble with the word "PR" is that it too often conjures up the image of a young girl handing out drinks at a function. So just what is meant when we talk about Public Relations? According to the Institute of Public Relations: "Public Relations is about reputation – the result of what you do, say and what others say about you. PR is the discipline which looks after the reputation, with the aim of earning understanding and support and influencing opinion and behaviour. It is the planned and sustained effort to establish and maintain goodwill and mutual understanding between an organisation and its public."

Sponsorship can play a vital role in providing a company with worthwhile PR opportunities. True, conventional advertising can be highly effective, otherwise companies wouldn't continue to spend hundreds of millions of pounds on it. The problem is that it is perceived by the public as being just that – paid-for advertising. It might create awareness, but there will always be a reluctance on the part of the public to believe everything that it states. On the other hand, if a newspaper carries an article about a product or company, the readership may believe what is being said is closer to the truth.

Sponsorship, used creatively, has the ability to provide a high level of feature-style media coverage. Imagine, for example, that as a result of some effective PR work by the marketing department of an international motorsport team, an article appeared in an in-flight airline magazine about Team Nasamax, explaining how it became the first team ever to complete the world famous Le Mans 24 Hours race, using a wholly renewable fuel – bio-ethanol. This would prove far more beneficial for the team's sponsors than if they had simply placed an advertisement in that publication.

PR can also play a pivotal role in helping to promote the Image Transfer that I have identified as being important to so many sponsors. Take the previous example. The airline magazine article on Team Nasamax would create the perception that "environmental awareness" is of importance to the sponsors of that team. This would be a direct result of Image Transfer. The team is concerned with the environment, therefore the sponsors of that team must also be concerned. This has been promoted because of the PR activity that enabled the article to appear in an airline magazine.

Other ways in which sponsorship can provide a host of excellent PR opportunities include:
• Media relations
• Newspapers (both national and local)
• TV, radio, magazines
• Corporate print: internal newsletters, press releases, reports
• Special events: conferences, exhibitions, product launches
• Photography: website, brochures

Promotions

The opportunity for a sponsor to create and implement special promotions, using the sponsorship as a platform, can often prove very important. These can range from in-store merchandising promotions to participative events linked to the sports programme itself. I remember Blackthorn (Cider), the main sponsor of Bath Rugby in the Zurich Premiership, devising a superb promotion called the Blackthorn Golden Boot Competition. It took place on a regional basis and its objective was to find the best goal-kicker in the region, outside of professional rugby. The competition took place at rugby union clubs throughout the region with the final taking place at half-time during one of Bath's televised matches at The Recreation Ground. The competition was promoted widely through all of the major retail outlets and supermarkets that stocked Blackthorn.

The great thing about creating innovative promotions on the back of a sponsorship is that for a sponsor, they take away much of the risk factor that comes from relying totally on the performance level of the sponsored team or individual. When I ran my own motor racing school at the Kyalami Grand Prix circuit in South Africa, I negotiated a sponsorship deal with Camel cigarettes. The way in which I put this together is detailed further on in the book. What it provided was the opportunity for Camel to run consumer promotions through many major retail store outlets, offering the public the chance to win places at the school and to participate in the Camel Rookie of the Year Challenge – in which they could win a test drive with the Paul Stewart racing team in the UK. It proved very popular.

The important thing to realise is that promotions don't have to be the sole preserve of large companies. Creating the opportunity of an innovative promotion for your local hardware store can be just as effective. Suppose the store agrees to sponsor a show jumper in a local event and has a product stall in place at the venue. By running a competition for a prize, comprising a course of riding lessons with coaching from the sponsored rider, the store could generate a useful database of names and addresses to which they could later send out special product offers and promotions.

The opportunities that sponsorship provides for creating innovative promotions is endless – and a very important factor when companies decide whether a sponsorship is cost effective.

Case study development

This is one of the most under-utilised reasons why a company will decide to become a sponsor, but it can be used very effectively. One of the first examples I came across of this was back in 1994/95, when Andersen Consulting (now Accenture) became an official sponsor of the Williams Formula 1 Team.

Accenture is a global management-consultancy, technology-services and outsourcing company – not exactly what you would think of as a typical Formula 1 sponsor. At that time, Williams were looking to move from their HQ at Didcot to a new state-of-the-art facility at Grove, near Wantage. This is not an easy thing for a Formula 1 Team to achieve without major disruption. Andersen Consulting saw an innovative opportunity to co-ordinate the move and help design the new factory; on that basis, they became an official sponsor of the team.

The effectiveness of the project management and lack of disruption caused by the move was demonstrated when Williams' F1 cars finished first and second in the season's opening race, going on to win both the Drivers' and Constructors' Championships. The project management of the move then provided Andersen Consulting with the ideal opportunity to produce a case study showing its involvement. This could then be used to promote the company's abilities to potential new clients.

It's not only in Formula 1 that such case studies can be effective. Take a small accountancy firm, for example. It might benefit from developing a case study on how it sponsors the local football team. This could show how it was able to introduce a far more effective way of handling the club's tax matters, saving it hundreds of pounds a year. The high local profile of the team might prove an effective point of interest for the firm to use the case study to generate new business in the area.

The opportunity that sponsorship can provide to develop powerful case study material is one that should not be overlooked. With a little bit of imagination, you should be able to come up with a number of possibilities for the use of this facet of sponsorship.

Business to business

The opportunity to generate business as a result of a sponsorship programme is a powerful reason for companies to participate in this form of marketing.

Never forget that the business world is fiercely competitive. Whatever message companies might like to portray, most of them are only interested in one thing – generating profit. It shouldn't come as a surprise then, when I tell you that in my experience most companies won't part with a penny of sponsorship money unless it directly or indirectly benefits their bottom line. Why should they? They have separate charity budgets for good causes. Sponsorship has to be justified for business reasons.

Unfortunately there are a lot of people who still think that sponsorship is their right. Because they happen to have won a particular championship or done well in whatever sport they are in, they think that it is now incumbent of companies to help them turn professional and make a career out of their sport. Although they will deny it until they are blue in the face, what they are in effect doing is seeking charity. You even hear it in some of the media interviews with the parents of talented young sports participants: "It's not fair, overseas youngsters get the backing of big business. We have to fork out money from our own pocket because companies here don't want to help."

Wrong! What these people really mean is that they don't know how to put forward a sponsorship proposal that shows a company how it can generate business through the use of a well thought-out sponsorship programme. I'm sure that many of you will know people who look upon sponsorship in this way. Unfortunately, when they look for sponsorship their primary objective is only too clear. They want to race a yacht in Cowes Week and they want someone else to pay for it, or they might want to row across the Atlantic single-handed, but want to do so at someone else's expense. The problem is not with this demand for sponsorship in itself, it's with the fact that, so often, little regard is given to the need for a commercial return for the sponsor.

Even at the top level of sport I've seen this happen. The management of a well-known professional rugby club looked upon sponsors as a necessary evil. They didn't want to give up the way that the club had been run in the amateur days – but were still more than happy to receive the fees that came with sponsorship. What came across was the perception that the least they had to do for the sponsors, the better. I remember seeing the team run out on to the pitch for one match at which one of the club's major sponsors was hosting a large hospitality function for their business clients. To the astonishment of everyone in that suite, the team was wearing shirts without the sponsor's branding. An unforgivable error that could have resulted in a lawsuit. Of course mistakes can happen, but the fact that no-one at the club really understood why the sponsor was so upset typified the problem.

Having talked about the need for a meaningful commercial return, this brings me to one of the most compelling reasons why a company decides to become a sponsor: the opportunity that it presents for securing meaningful business-to-business revenue. Put very simply, if it can be shown to the board members or owner of a company that by spending £25,000 on a sponsorship programme with a sports team, the company should be able to generate at least £50,000 of business from other commercial sponsors of the team, the proposal will most likely be of some interest. Needless to say, it isn't always that straightforward, but the principle is important. Every company looks to expand its customer base and to increase turnover and profit. If it doesn't, it will soon go out of business.

If you can show the senior executives of a company that through the innovative use of sports sponsorship it can generate additional business, you stand a good chance of at least securing a meeting. Imagine you are the marketing manager of a cricket team. You're seeking a sponsor for an overseas tour in the off-season. Your team already has a major sponsor in place. It's a company called Markhams, specialising in building and civil engineering. Markhams won't extend its sponsorship agreement to cover the proposed tour, but after a conversation with its managing director, you gain agreement for a strategy that might pay dividends in identifying a company that will.

Your first step is to approach your local motor dealership and meet with the sales director to present the tour sponsorship opportunity. In the process, you mention that following a discussion with the MD of Markhams, the club's existing sponsor, it has come to light that the company runs a fleet of 15 company cars, which it buys from another dealership. These vehicles are changed every two years.

You go on to explain to the sales director that even if his dealership decides to sponsor the tour, there is no way that you can guarantee it will secure this future vehicle business from Markhams. However, what you can guarantee is that if the sponsorship is agreed, the Markhams' MD will immediately set up a meeting with the dealership's sales director to discuss the potential future purchase of cars.

In other words, what you are offering is the guarantee of a meeting at the right level, but not of business. That will only come if the dealership is able to put forward a convincing business case. However, that presents the dealership with a very real business opportunity and might be enough, in addition with the other sponsorship entitlements, to persuade it to accept your proposal.

This is a very simplistic example. The main point is that you are offering a potential business-to-business opportunity, which uses the sponsorship as a catalyst. It should not be difficult to understand why business-to-business is a major factor in the decision-making process of many companies.

One of the largest sponsorship deals that I ever generated was with FedEx, whom I secured as a major sponsor for the Benetton Formula 1 Team. I was able to show this company the tremendous business opportunities that could open up within the Benetton Group of companies if they became a sponsor of the F1 team. In addition, there would also be other opportunities to meet the key decision-makers within some of the other 40-odd sponsors and suppliers of the Benetton F1 Team. Although it wasn't the only reason they signed up, it did play a major role in the decision-making process.

One thing that I should emphasise is to never promise potential business. As the example showed, the most that you can normally offer is the chance of a meeting with key personnel who would be in a position to make decisions. In most cases that is enough. Companies will recognise that it is then up to their own sales skills to secure a business relationship. The chance of a meeting at the right level, in favourable circumstances, can be a tempting opportunity.

Community involvement

Many companies are keen to build a good relationship with the local community in which they operate and use sponsorship for this purpose. They realise the importance this can have in terms of recruitment, as well as perhaps maintaining a good working relationship with the local council, which can help in matters such as future planning applications.

I have found this to be the case on many occasions. I negotiated a substantial sponsorship with Virgin Mobile on behalf of Bath Rugby Union Club, based on the fact that the Virgin Mobile Head Office was in the same geographical region and employed over 1,400 people from that area. They saw the importance of being involved with a team that enjoyed the support of many of their work force and which was itself involved in working with the local community through its schools programme.

Wolverhampton Wanderers, the football team that I have always supported, was sponsored by Goodyear Tyre Company for many years. Its head office was then at Bushbury, about five miles away from Wolves' Molineux Stadium. Goodyear even had its own hospitality suite at Molineux so that it could entertain its own staff at matches, in addition to its corporate hospitality activities. The opportunity for a company to be seen to play a role in the local community can be high up on their list of reasons for becoming a sponsor.

Sales incentives

Although some companies use sponsorship for this reason, I am surprised that this hasn't been taken on board by a lot more. I mentioned earlier that I had worked for Rank Xerox. They were great believers in innovative sales incentive programmes to motivate their substantial sales force. On one occasion, I was invited along with the other 999 salespeople that worked there to a sales conference at the Drury Lane Theatre in London's West End. At this conference, the announcement was made about the annual sales incentive programme for the forthcoming year. It was called the Race of Champions and was based on a Formula 1 Grand Prix season. The opportunity existed for salespeople to win interim prizes at different stages of the 12-month programme. These prizes normally involved trips to UK motor races and some overseas Grands Prix.

Following this, the Chairman announced the top prize, which would go to the overall winner of the Race of Champions at the end of the 12-month competition. To everyone's amazement, Stirling Moss drove it onto the stage. It was a brand new MGB GT V8. At that time, it was worth a lot of money.

A well-structured sponsorship programme can be used as a highly-effective platform for the design and implementation of such an incentive programme for a company's sales force. If you have targeted a company that employs a reasonably high number of salespeople and you can build an innovative sales incentive programme into your sponsorship proposal, you will immediately be head and shoulders above your competitors. For the right company, sales incentive programmes are extremely important and the opportunity to create a scheme around a sports sponsorship can be highly attractive.

Personal appearances by sports personalities

One of the factors that contribute to a company sponsoring an individual or a team is the opportunity to invite a sports personality to major business events. These might be sales conferences, exhibitions, product launches, client presentations or even an exclusive business dinner with a VIP client.

The bigger the name, the more attractive this is, but don't underestimate the value that any level of sportsperson might offer. It is relative to the size of a company and the importance of that person to its target market; the chance for a company to invite the winner of a local, but high-profile cycle race to open a new shop may be important. Alternatively, the opportunity to invite a VIP client to play a round of golf with the captain of the local football team can also be very effective. If a sponsor is able to build into a sponsorship agreement the right to a specified number of days with the sponsored individual or team member, it can provide a significant reason for going ahead with the proposed deal.

Brand value through advertising

Many companies will consider sponsorship because of the opportunity it provides to further demonstrate brand values through the use of that sponsorship in its conventional advertising. In America, this has been used extensively for much longer than here in the UK. Sponsors in the NASCAR championship exploit this opportunity and you will see their print-media advertising and TV commercials using their sponsorship involvement to add power to the brand.

What sponsorship can do is provide a powerful, personal communication link between a company's advertising and its target market. The sponsorship of a major sporting event, for example, will allow the public to feel closer to the sponsoring company, and vice versa, in a way that doesn't happen with conventional advertising. This can be an important consideration in the use of sports sponsorship.

Merchandising

For an appropriate company, the opportunity to develop a range of branded merchandise, such as t-shirts, caps and bags, can be very attractive. This form of marketing is often used to help promote the launch of a new product or brand. An innovative sports sponsorship programme can provide an effective platform for this to generate a higher degree of interest than if it were simply product-based. Although this is perhaps more effective for larger companies, there is no reason why merchandising can't play an important role at any level of a sponsorship programme.

It is quite normal for sponsors to insist on the right to use the team's or association's badge/brand in association with their own brand identity on a range of merchandise. The more well-known the badge, the more effective this link becomes for the sponsor.

Product sampling

This can be a very powerful marketing tool for a company. Suppose that you are staging a sporting event at a stadium. Provided you have the rights to do this, you can show a potential sponsor that they can hand out free product samples to each person who goes through the turnstiles. This can be every effective for a company producing soft drinks, or biscuits, or anything that they want to put straight into the hands of the general public. On its own, it won't be the reason why they sponsor, but in addition to other factors, it can be a very important issue. If you look at the last case study, SodaStream, you'll see how I used this as an important part of a successful sponsorship proposal.

Recruitment

I remember at the time being very surprised when two global companies, with whom I worked closely, told me that one of the major reasons why they used motorsport sponsorship was to promote recruitment. In a highly competitive market, they wanted to attract the very best graduates and they found that their involvement in motorsport was very often a powerful influence. They found that it showed the graduates that the company was forward thinking and young in nature, qualities that were perceived as being important. The two companies were Honda and Nissan.

You'll learn in another of the case studies in the book how recruitment was the main reason for a British company to enter into a sponsorship agreement with a top speedway team. This factor is very rarely used in sponsorship decision-making and yet you'll see how effective it can be for a company.

As I stressed at the beginning of this chapter, these are just a few of the reasons why a company will consider including sponsorship in their marketing mix. It is rare for there to be only one factor that generates interest and most sponsorships are concluded through a combination of several of these.

It's important to be aware of these factors. If you are, you can develop your sponsorship opportunity to provide a range of entitlements that will build a much stronger case than if you simply rely on brand awareness and hospitality. These two criteria are vital to many prospective sponsors and your competitors in the search for sponsorship will almost certainly be offering opportunities for achieving them. However, they may not have put forward many of the other opportunities which have been identified. By incorporating these into sponsorship proposals, it can make a great difference to a company's interest in accepting your proposals.

SUMMARY

If you don't understand the reasons why companies use sports sponsorship as an important part of their marketing strategies, you will find it extremely difficult to match the features of your sponsorship opportunity to their marketing requirements. Although the need for brand awareness and hospitality are two important reasons why companies sponsor, there is a long list of other factors that can be equally, if not more important.

The more options you have to offer, the more likely you are to structure a sponsorship proposal that will meet a company's needs. There are many reasons why companies sponsor, including some of these:

- Brand awareness
- Business-to-business opportunities
- Community involvement
- Sales incentives
- Case study development
- Integration with advertising
- Personal appearances
- Merchandising
- Product sampling
- Recruitment
- Hospitality
- Image transfer.

Arbuthnot Latham

About Arbuthnot Latham

Arbuthnot Latham provides a high-quality and personalised wealth management service, aimed at attracting successful private and corporate clients, including entrepreneurs and high-earning professionals. Arbuthnot is part of the highly successful Secure Trust Banking Group plc, listed on the London Stock Exchange.

The Arbuthnot Latham companies provide banking, foreign exchange, corporate finance, pensions, financial planning, insurance, investment management, trust management and factoring services to professional firms, owner-managed companies, charities, pension funds and individuals.

The Arbuthnot name has been associated with banking for over 170 years and today retains its traditional qualities, personalised service and relationship banking.

Case study

It is often said that the hardest person to sell a sports sponsorship opportunity to, is one who is passionate about the sport that you are presenting. A classic example of this is was when John Reed, the CEO of Arbuthnot Latham, was presented with the opportunity for his bank to become the title sponsor of the Historic Grand Prix Cars Association.

As a keen racer himself, competing in the highly competitive Radical Sportscar series, John is only too aware of how easy it can be for a company to participate as a sponsor for all the wrong reasons. His experience had shown him, however, that it could also be a highly effective business tool, if used correctly and innovatively.

In his role as CEO, John is always open to opportunities for the development of future business. Having seen, with his previous bank, that motor-racing sponsorship could be helpful in both identifying and introducing high-worth individuals, he was aware that this could also work well for Arbuthnot Latham.

Although the Bank hadn't previously been involved in any form of sports sponsorship, there was an interesting link with motorsport. Long before the advent of commercial sponsorship, back in the 1930s, Robert Michael Arbuthnot, a member of the family that founded the bank, raced an Alfa Romeo car at the famous Brooklands circuit, winning the coveted Campbell Trophy with a new class record in the last race before World War II stopped play.

Together with his colleagues, John Reed identified four areas of motorsport that presented Arbuthnot Latham with the potential for business, both medium- and long-term:

1. The young drivers who would progress through the various disciplines in motorsport to ultimately become high-earners in their own right. If they could be identified early on in their careers, and an association or relationship formed, there was a good possibility that they would become valuable clients of the bank in future years. Indeed, many of them already come from fairly wealthy backgrounds, to be able to afford even a modest level of competition in karting and junior categories of the sport in the first place.

2. Professional drivers already at the level where they are earning multi-million pound fees. This might include Formula 1, World Rallying and other top categories of the sport. It has to be said that John Reed does not perceive this as being the key market, because by the time a driver reaches this level, he is being courted by so many institutions, that there is little margin for profitable business to be achieved. The main benefit, if it were to happen, would be from a PR perspective, using the media coverage that can be derived from an involvement with a star name.

3. Those who can best be described as gentlemen drivers. These are considered to be the perfect client for Arbuthnot Latham. They are usually high-net-worth individuals, many of them well known in business and society circles, who have an absolute passion for racing or driving exotic, historic racing cars. Such people are normally very successful and wealthy in their own right.

4. Teams and suppliers within the motorsport industry. Many of these companies are owned privately by individuals, while others are limited companies. Both of these categories fit well with the target market that Arbuthnot Latham is interested in working with. Many companies within the industry are relatively small, but have the same banking requirements as in any other business sector.

The first step in developing the strategy was to launch The Arbuthnot Latham Motorsport Partnership. This is a specialist motorsport team, dedicated to the management of the financial affairs of those involved in motorsport. It comprises banking, investment and wealth management professionals, each with a passion and understanding for all things "motorsport". In addition to this, membership of the Motorsport Partnership offers access to a number of other services such as legal, accountancy, taxation and management advice. The thinking behind the launch of this initiative was that it could provide a service to all four sectors of the target market that are outlined above.

This enabled Arbuthnot Latham to create an internal structure that was capable of exploiting the potential such a partnership could offer. It also allowed the bank to consider the possibility of Arbuthnot Latham becoming a sponsor within motorsport, as the structure that had been put in place would be capable of supporting such an involvement, from a personnel point of view.

The next question was what would be the best way of using sponsorship to complement the Motorsport Partnership initiative?

It was decided by the Motorsport Partnership team that historic racing offered the greatest opportunity for a number of reasons. This sector of motorsport is becoming extremely popular worldwide, and it was decided by John Reed and his team that it offered a number of specific benefits to Arbuthnot Latham. These included:

Image transfer
The perception of historic racing offers a number of qualities that would provide a perfect match for the qualities that Arbuthnot Latham would like to be associated with. These included:

• Tradition
• Fun
• Quality
• Sportsmanship

- Fair play
- Team spirit
- Camaraderie
- Competitiveness
- Co-operation
- Classic values.

Access
The arrangement allowed for the Arbuthnot Latham motorsport team to form close personal relationships with the association's 300-350 high-net-worth membership. The intention was to convert some of these personal relationships into direct business relationships over time.

Brand awareness
The opportunity within motorsport for developing brand awareness relevant to Arbuthnot's target socio-economic group is greater than in many other sports.

Hospitality
This would provide the opportunity to develop closer relationships with existing clients who had expressed an interest in motorsport, as well as creating new associations. It would also allow an opportunity for face-to-face meetings on a social level, between senior Arbuthnot Latham personnel and clients.

To summarise
The main criteria that would be looked for in a sponsorship opportunity would be:
- Image transfer
- Access
- Brand awareness
- Hospitality.

The sponsorship
The Historic Grand Prix Cars Association's approach to Arbuthnot Latham for sponsorship coincided with the decision by John Reed and his team to expand its use of motorsport. Research had shown that historic racing in the UK exceeded Formula 1 in terms of turnover and its contribution to UK GNP. At the pinnacle of historic racing are the Grand Prix cars of yesteryear and the premier international organisation for owning and racing such cars is the HGPCA. This organisation stages events for cars dating from 1920 through to 1966. For Arbuthnot Latham, the fit with the HGPCA was deemed appropriate and John Reed subsequently concluded a sponsorship deal with the association.

The agreement that Arbuthnot Latham entered into with the HGPCA was designed to foster a close working relationship between the bank, their private clients and the members of the association.

The fee
Although the sponsorship fee involved must remain confidential, it is worth noting that instead of agreeing to the full original request of the HGPCA, Arbuthnot Latham proposed an innovative alternative. Instead of providing the association solely with a cash payment as proposed, John Reed was able to convince the Association that far greater value could be delivered by the payment of a lesser fee, but with the added value of benefits that could offer far greater returns for their members.

This included the provision of a 42inch plasma screen and audio-visual system that would enable the in-car camera footage to be played back in the hospitality area at the end of the races. Arbuthnot Latham also provided these in-car race cams. This has proved exceptionally entertaining for all of the competitors and hospitality guests alike. It has the added attraction to the bank of ensuring that everyone gathers in the hospitality area at the end of the meeting rather than rushing off. In this way, the Arbuthnot Latham personnel achieve their objective of face-to-face meetings, albeit in a social context rather than a business one.

The footage from the car cams would be edited so that everyone could have a copy, and could be used at the end of the year awards presentation. In this way, Arbuthnot Latham has added considerable weight to the interest levels in the racing with several other elements to the package including co-branded clothing, paddock scooters, mobile internet access and catering support which have all helped reinforce the feeling of adding real value.

Period of agreement

The sponsorship that was agreed was for a three-year period. In this way, both parties benefit. Arbuthnot Latham can use the first year to effectively learn the ropes and understand how the HGPCA operates. It can also start to develop good working relationships with the people involved. In the second year the bank can build on this and look at ways of further cementing the relationship and effecting additional benefits from the sponsorship.

Measurement

Because Arbuthnot Latham see the relationship with the HGPCA as being long rather than short-term, it is still early days in terms of introducing measurement guidelines that will demonstrate the success or otherwise of this sponsorship.

Ways in which measurement will ultimately be applied include:
• The number of new accounts that have been opened with clients, emanating in some way from the motorsport initiatives
• The number of young drivers (and wealthy parents) attracted to use the bank's services
• The number of teams and suppliers that become clients of the bank
• The number of gentleman racers that become clients.

Author's comments

1. Arbuthnot Latham have approached the sponsorship of the HGPCA in a structured, but innovative, manner. The creation of a team within the bank to work with clients and potential clients appears to be extremely effective. The bank has sensibly looked upon the first year of this three-year agreement as being very much a learning curve. It has realised that a fairly low-key approach is very much in line with the nature of its potential clients who are involved in this championship.

2. Having become a major sponsor in international motorsport, Arbuthnot Latham is regularly approached by sponsorship seekers from a range of sports. The feeling within the bank is that very few of the proposals received are based on ideas that might help the bank generate business, either short or long-term. Too many are simply pleas for assistance, albeit very professionally presented ones in terms of appearance and material. Few have really shown any evidence of understanding why a bank of Arbuthnot's status would chose to use sports sponsorship as a marketing tool.

Chapter 5

A saleable sponsorship **property**

Those of you who like cooking will be only too aware that the key to producing a successful meal is the standard of preparation you undertake. The same rule could equally apply to the business of securing a commercial sponsor. The better the quality of your preparation, the more likely you are to be successful.

It doesn't matter whether you're looking for £500 or £500,000. If you put in the right amount of quality groundwork, you'll not only develop so much more confidence in your ability to interest companies in what you have to offer, but you'll save yourself a lot of time further down the road.

If you want an analogy with sport, you only have to look at Michael Schumacher. His achievement in winning a record number of Formula 1 World Championships is quite extraordinary, but he would be the first to admit that it is not solely based on his superb ability to drive his Ferrari at race-winning pace. It is a combination of a number of factors, but very often it is the Ferrari race strategy that helps Michael win races, supported by his ability to put in incredibly quick laps to help make the strategy work. A lot of his success is due to the team's ability to adapt a race strategy quicker and more effectively than his rivals. This can be put down to the tremendous amount of preparation that both Michael and his team undertake to provide themselves with a wide range of options when it really matters.

Sponsorship seeking is very similar. The reaction of companies to a sponsorship proposal can be extremely unpredictable. As a result, you need to prepare for as many eventualities as you can. It's rather like setting out on a long journey in your car. You can't always predict major traffic hold-ups, emergency road works or accidents, but if you have a map with you, it's usually possible to find a detour that will eventually get you back on the main route to your destination. Without that map you are more than likely to experience a problem. A strategy is like a map and should help you reach your destination in the easiest way.

You may think that it's not feasible to develop such a strategy because every approach that you make to a company will be different. You may also feel that a strategy would be too restricting. While I would agree with you that every company is different and has its own individual needs, I don't agree that this means that you can't develop a meaningful sales plan.

A well-thought-out strategy will provide you with the very flexibility that is essential if you're to adapt to changing situations. The reason that Michael Schumacher is able to adapt so effectively is because he knows at any time in a Grand Prix exactly where he is in relation to his strategy. That provides him with a sound platform on which to make appropriate decisions and still achieve his aim of winning the race.

The strategy that I want you to consider is not hugely complex. It is based on the logical steps that you really need to go through in preparing to market your sponsorship opportunity. In many walks of life, we are all guilty of charging off like the proverbial bull in a china shop when we get an idea in our head about something. We rush off, full of enthusiasm and good intentions, only to suddenly come up against an unexpected obstacle which completely throws us. Had we sat down and thought about what we were going to do for a few minutes, we could have

"You're not going to win a marathon if you haven't put in the groundwork. It's the same with sponsorship"

easily foreseen the problems that might come up and considered ways of either avoiding or dealing with them.

It's the same with sponsorship. When you first decide to approach companies, it's likely that your enthusiasm will carry you forward. The problems come after your fifth or sixth rejection. You suddenly run out of steam, the enthusiasm declines and you are not sure what to do next. The positive reaction that you anticipated hasn't materialised and all sorts of objections are being thrown at you that you have no answer for.

Don't worry, it has happened to most of us! There is nothing wrong with enthusiasm. Just the opposite in fact; enthusiasm is one of the greatest attributes that you can have in this business. One of the most powerful comments that I have ever heard on the subject came from a training officer at the Rank Xerox sales training school that I attended all those years ago:

"There is only one thing more contagious than enthusiasm: a total lack of it."

Think about it. How true that is. I remember at school that there were some teachers who just didn't seem to have any enthusiasm for their subject and it rubbed off on everyone in the class. My history teacher was a classic example and I hated history as a result. Yet today, historical research is one of my greatest loves in life.

What I am saying is that it's fine to be enthusiastic, but you need to control and channel that enthusiasm, in order to make the best use of it. Before reaching for the phone and calling half a dozen companies that come to mind, you need to plan a course of action. I have always found that the best way of achieving this is to spend some time developing a simple but effective sponsorship sales strategy document. This will be your road map. What you will be doing is to put down on paper the various steps that you will need to go through to reach the point where you agree a sponsorship deal with a prospect. I know this is alien to many people who just want to get out into the marketplace and get selling.

I can assure you that if you adopt this approach, you'll develop the same confidence that an athlete gains from knowing he or she has trained and prepared better than his opposition. As with sport, there is a definite link between confidence and success. Expect to be successful and you are more likely to be so. This only works, however, if your expectation is based on sound logic. You're not going to win a marathon if you haven't put in the groundwork, however hard you might try to believe that you can. It's the same with sponsorship. Put in the preparation and the confidence will follow.

Having hopefully convinced you of the need to develop a sales strategy, I want to outline the way that I go about creating one. What I am in effect going to do is to break the sales process down into a number of steps, which will logically take me from A to Z. A is the point at which you decide you need sponsorship for whatever reason. Z is the point at which you have a signed agreement in your hand.

If you use a written format to do this, it will make the task much easier and you will have a document to refer back to and also to amend as needed.

There is no better place to start than right at the beginning. You have decided that for whatever reason you need sports sponsorship.

Perhaps you have decided that you need to move up a gear in the sport in which you participate and have come to the conclusion that you will need sponsorship to help you achieve this. It could be that you work for a rugby team and have been asked to find a replacement sponsor for one that has just pulled out. Alternatively, you could be working for a sports marketing agency and have been given the task of securing sponsorship for a new event for which the agency has just acquired the marketing rights. In other words, you are starting from scratch.

In the previous chapter, we examined the main reasons why a company uses sponsorship as an effective marketing tool. In a perfect world, you would now prepare a sponsorship proposal that meets every one of these factors, contact a company and have them biting your hand off for a chance to sign a sponsorship deal with you. In the real world, there is a lot of work to do before you reach that stage and the first important step is to create a product that is saleable.

What exactly do I mean by that? Of course my sponsorship opportunity is saleable, you're probably thinking. Are you sure? Just as you would find it extremely difficult to sell a right-hand drive car in a left-hand drive country, so you will find it almost impossible to sell a sponsorship opportunity that is priced wrongly and doesn't offer any meaningful benefits. So the first step in your sales strategy is:

Create a saleable property

You must have watched some of the seemingly endless number of house makeover programmes that grace our TV screens. Several of these deal with the subject of selling a house. I must admit to being surprised to learn that there are now people who make a living from advising house-sellers on how to prepare their house to sell quickly and for a higher price than they expected. But they do come up with all sorts of important tips that can make the house look more attractive, including ways of creating the illusion of it being lighter and more spacious.

These experts will tell you that you shouldn't rely on the vision of a potential buyer in seeing beyond the clutter and unimaginative decoration that so many properties seem to offer. My wife is very different from me when we look at houses. She can immediately see beyond the tacky wallpaper or the hanging chandeliers and imagine what the room could look like if it were painted white, if concealed lighting was installed and if a wall was knocked down, making two rooms into one. I don't have that ability.

The same principle applies to selling a sponsorship proposal. When you approach companies, don't rely on the vision of their marketing management to identify all the different ways in which they could exploit your sponsorship property and make it work for them. In my experience, there are far too many people working in the marketing departments of some major companies that quite frankly wouldn't recognise the deal of the century if it stared them in the face. Vision and creativity are not always found in abundance in the corporate world. It's up to you to spell it out for them, chapter and verse. In other words, make your property as attractive as possible by illustrating all of the various features that it can offer. Don't expect potential buyers to work them out for themselves. In other words, you need to create a saleable property.

How do you do this with a sponsorship opportunity? The first step is to identify as many features as possible that your "property" can offer:

Features

The more features that your sponsorship opportunity can offer potential sponsors, the more likely you are to identify some that appeal to them. This is where you'll need to be very creative and imaginative. It might be advantageous to enlist the help of some friends or business colleagues in the task.

Start with a completely blank sheet of paper. Write down every single entitlement (or "feature") that you think your sponsorship opportunity can offer. And I mean everything! It doesn't matter how important or unimportant they might seem to you, write them down. This is where it will help to get a few other people to sit around a table with you. Four brains are often better than

"The marketing departments of some major companies wouldn't recognise the deal of the century if it stared them in the face"

one and between you there is a good chance that you'll all come up with some really thought provoking ideas.

To help you in this task, I've put together an example. A motorsport club is seeking a sponsor for its club championship. The person who has been handed the responsibility for securing this funding has enlisted the help of a couple of other club members and done exactly what I've suggested you do. Together they have come up with a list of as many entitlements as possible that they can offer:

• Sponsor's brand in championship title
• Sponsor's brand on front of the official programme for each round
• Sponsor's advert in the programme
• Sponsor's brand on each car in the championship
• Trackside signage
• Announcements on PA system at each round
• Sponsor's brand on tickets
• Official press launch for sponsor
• Driver appearances at sponsor events
• Complimentary tickets
• Sponsor on-track promotions
• Sponsor off-track promotions
• Product sampling opportunities
• Exclusivity of category (prevents competitive sponsors)
• Open day at track mid-week
• Community relationship/local school/college
• Right to develop case study
• Right to use photographs in sponsor's advertising
• Copyright-free photographs
• Press releases
• Use of a show car

- Right to develop merchandise with club/sponsor logo
- The opportunity to distribute sponsor's promotions to the club's database
- VIP hospitality
- Possible media partner (e.g. local radio station)
- Structured networking events
- Introduction to all local media
- Sponsorship of podium backdrop
- Sponsorship of branded trophies
- Circuit tours
- Adverts in the club magazine
- TV coverage of selected events on regional news programmes
- Test day hospitality
- Free circuit parking.

This list could almost certainly be extended to include many more potential entitlements, but it should give you an idea of what you can do with a little thought. There is probably nothing in the list that will surprise you, but the point that I want to make is that although you might be aware of all these items, the potential sponsor may well not be. Even entitlements that might seem obvious to you, such as the opportunity for free parking, can be a major factor to the potential sponsor. You should never pre-judge what is or isn't important to the prospective sponsor, or what they believe they can receive as part of their package.

By going through the discipline of listing all of these points, no matter how minor, you'll ensure you bring them all into your proposal and in the process, make the sponsorship opportunity as attractive as you can. Remember the house sale story. Don't rely on the buyers' vision. Spell it out for them.

The next step in the process is to sort each one of these entitlements under a number of category headings. I usually find that the best way of doing this is to work from the list of reasons that we looked at earlier as to why companies sponsor. Your headings might then include: brand awareness, hospitality, image transfer, PR, promotions, business-to-business, case studies, incentive programmes, community relationships and product sampling.

Once you've done this, go through your list of entitlements, decide which category they should fall under and write them down accordingly. When you've completed this, leave it for a couple of days and then go back to it and see if you can come up with even more. With some real imagination, you'll be surprised at just what you are actually able to offer a potential sponsor. It will be a lot more than you initially considered.

By adopting this approach, you'll find it far easier to find features of your sponsorship property that can satisfy the needs of the sponsor. This is particularly true if it becomes apparent that brand awareness and hospitality will not be enough on their own. What you are doing is creating a far more saleable product.

There is another very important reason for putting together such a list. It will help you arrive at a realistic valuation of the sponsorship opportunity that you are marketing. That is extremely important and is a practice that a lot of sponsorship-seekers ignore.

So often I have heard them talk about the fee they have placed on their opportunity and yet when they are asked how they arrived at that fee, they haven't got a clue. The usual response is to embark on a list of all the costs that they will incur during the delivery of that sponsorship. If it costs them £50,000 to compete in the World Karting Championships, then that must be the value of the sponsorship opportunity. That's not the right way to go about it!

This is such an important area that I want to spend some more time examining this vital part of creating a saleable property.

Valuation

Have you ever sold a car? I don't mean a new one, but one that you've owned yourself for a while. When you decided to advertise it, can you remember the price you set? How did you arrive at that figure? I would hazard a guess that it was probably with the help of the price guides that you find in the back of magazines such as What Car or Auto Trader. In other words, you checked the going rate for your particular model, taking into account the mileage and its condition. You may have had to come down slightly on the price that you expected in order to close a deal, but the chances are that if you did your homework carefully, you wouldn't have found it too difficult to sell.

You now have to do exactly the same with your sponsorship opportunity, if you are to have a saleable property. If you don't set the price fairly accurately, one of two things will happen: you'll never sell it or you'll sell it for much less than it is worth.

The problem is that while you can fairly easily find out what the market value of your car is, it is far more difficult to arrive at a market value for your sponsorship opportunity. Perhaps that's why I have found that this is an area so often overlooked when approaching companies.

Imagine that you have succeeded in setting up a meeting with a company to outline your sponsorship proposal. Into the boardroom walk two people.

One is the marketing manager and the other is the financial controller. After you have run through your initial presentation and had a reasonable discussion with the marketing person, he asks you how much the sponsorship will cost him. You reply with the figure that you've decided upon. Nothing too difficult as yet, you're thinking.

The financial controller asks a question for the first time: "How did you arrive at that figure?"

Unfortunately this is where a lot of people then start to defend their position by explaining how expensive it is to either run their race car or travel to all the rounds of their clay-pigeon shooting championships, or whatever. In other words, what they are doing is confusing cost with value.

There is a critical difference between the two, although sometimes they might both have the same monetary amount. Let me explain.

Two speedway riders, Grant and Darren, of similar ability on the track, are going to compete in all nine rounds of the Speedway Grand Prix Championship, which involves racing in nine different countries. They are both seeking sponsorship. They have both put together proposals and decided on the fees that they will request.

Grant's operational plan for the season includes staying at five-star hotels, flying to each venue and employing six mechanics to service his bikes and transport them from event to event. He has costed the season at £150,000, so that is the fee he attached to his sponsorship proposal.

Darren, on the other hand, has decided to use a camper van for the season and make do with just four mechanics. He has costed the season at £90,000 and that is the fee that he decides to ask for.

Both riders contact the same company and submit their proposals. So what do we have from a sponsor's point of view? Same series, same opportunities and entitlements, same media coverage, same hospitality, but two fees that vary by a huge amount, simply because of the different levels of cost involved. They can't both be correct.

After carefully looking at the opportunity and involving his sponsorship evaluation personnel, the prospective sponsor decides that it is worth around £75,000 to his company, based on other comparative sponsorship opportunities that exist in the market place and comparisons to conventional advertising. The question is then asked as to why two almost identical opportunities should vary so much in respect of the fee expected?

The answer is actually very simple. They vary because both riders have misunderstood the fact that what is important to the potential sponsor is not what it costs them to compete in the Championship, but what the value of that opportunity is to the company. Their predicted costs of participation have varied greatly, but the value of the sponsorship opportunity is exactly the same in both cases.

At this point, I am sure that there are many of you who will take the view that the value of the sponsorship property is whatever you can get for it. For example, if you can get a £75,000 fee for a sponsorship programme that should be valued at around £40,000, isn't that a great deal?

The answer to that question depends on whether you are looking very short-term or whether you are keen to build a long-term relationship with a sponsor. What is likely to happen if you do secure this type of deal? However unlikely you may think it is, there is a very strong chance that at some stage through the season, your sponsor will get into conversation with another sponsor in the same sport. Being business people, the subject of value for money will probably arise. When your sponsor realises that he has paid over the odds for what he is getting, he will not be too happy and the chances of him ultimately renewing the agreement will be very slim. If you do lose that sponsor, you will also have lost a good point of testimonial reference for the future. Companies that you might contact to replace that sponsor at the end of the agreement will most likely want to know how the previous sponsorship worked out and why that company didn't continue its relationship with you. One phone call to the MD of the previous sponsor could spell disaster for your chances of being successful.

If you want to work on that basis, that's up to you, but remember that people talk and if you develop a reputation for not giving value for money, it will harm your future prospects.

So if the value of the sponsorship to a company does not necessarily correlate with the cost of participation, how do you arrive at that valuation? There is no simple formula that will provide this. The good news, however, is that the work that you have hopefully done in preparing a list of all the entitlements you are able to offer will play an important role. What you need to do is to work your way through that list and identify all the entitlements that you can put a price to.

For example, if you are offering hospitality for six people at each event, you can put a specific figure against that based on what it would cost the company if they had to pay for it themselves. Similarly, you may have included a one-page advertisement in the official programme for each event. You can find out what that would cost the sponsor if it had to be paid for.

After applying this to all the "priceable" entitlements, you need to look at what remains and estimate a value for these items. Suppose that you've guaranteed a feature article in the local newspaper. You should be able to determine an approximate value for this based on what it would cost the company to place an advertorial of the same size. The paper's sales department will give you the price for this.

As another example, you might have included in your sponsorship proposal, an entitlement for one of your team's star players to attend three business functions during the year for the sponsor. You should be able to ascertain what this would cost if you contact a professional speakers agency and identify speakers of similar status and ask what their fee would be to attend a similar type of function. These don't have to be precise figures, but if you can get a fairly accurate estimate of likely costs in this way, it will help you arrive at a realistic fee valuation for your sponsorship property.

The next step is to try to compare your sponsorship opportunity with others that are either currently available, or which have been successfully implemented. This will obviously involve finding out the fee that was paid in each case. This isn't always easy, but it is important if you are going to pitch your opportunity at the right level. You need to know what is being paid by companies for similar sponsorship deals.

Your sports governing body or association may well be able to give you some guidance as to what are realistic fees within your own sport. There are also many publications that specialise in the sports marketing field and provide details of many of the sponsorship deals as they are negotiated. These include SportBusiness International and Sponsorship News, as well as specialist sports media magazines and websites relating to your own sport.

Although some of your fellow competitors may be willing to advise you on what they have secured in sponsorship, be careful with this, because egos will come into play and you may get highly exaggerated claims.

If you have any friends in the advertising or marketing agency sector, ask them to help you on this. Outline your sponsorship opportunity and ask them to get it valued for you. It might come as a shock when they tell you the real value, but it's better to know at this stage than when you are sitting in front of your sponsorship prospect.

If you adopt the approach that I've just outlined, you should be able to arrive at what is a reasonable estimate of the true value of your sponsorship opportunity. It is a blend of the actual

"Remember that people talk and if you develop a reputation for not giving value for money, it will harm your future prospects"

entitlement values and the value that comes from all of the qualities that sponsorship is able to offer, which in general can't be derived from conventional advertising.

It's difficult to put a value on qualities such as aspiration or team building which we've seen come under the heading of Image Transfer. Don't worry too much about that. The very fact that you have identified that there is a value for these qualities, over and above the value placed on all the other entitlements, shows that you have structured the fee in a professional and not haphazard manner. You will be far more likely, as a result, to gain the respect of that financial controller when he asks you how you arrived at your sponsorship fee.

You've now created a sponsorship property that should have a wide appeal, with a comprehensive range of entitlements, and which is priced both competitively and realistically. The first step in developing your sales strategy is now in place.

SUMMARY

The phenomenal success of Michael Schumacher is not only due to his exceptional driving talent. It is also based on the design and adherence to a carefully planned strategy that is flexible and capable of maximising his skills.

Knowing what you are doing at any stage of the sponsorship sales process will increase your confidence greatly and reduce your fear of the unknown. The first step in the sales strategy is to make sure that you create a sponsorship property that is saleable, through the inclusion of a wide range of potential benefits to the target market. The sponsorship fee should be based on market value and not on the cost of participation. It needs to be competitive and realistic.

Unless you know how you have arrived at your sponsorship fee and can justify it to a potential sponsor, you are going to run into problems in the presentation of your sponsorship opportunity.

It's not a benefit **until they tell you so**

When I started my motor racing career, I have to admit that one of the things that attracted me to it was the glamour. I'd watched Grand Prix drivers such as Jochen Rindt, Jackie Stewart, Jo Siffert and Mike Hailwood racing at the British Grand Prix in the days when the venue for this prestigious event alternated every year between Brands Hatch and Silverstone. In that era, you could get really close to the drivers and teams in the paddock, and I noticed that there was never a shortage of stunning girls in the vicinity of these intrepid Formula 1 pilots.

My own career was starting to move along quite well and I was competing in Formula Ford 1600. At that time, it was the only junior formula to be in. Formula Renault, BMW, Vauxhall, Opel and all the myriad formulae that have, in my opinion, totally overloaded the motorsport structure, were still unheard of. Formula Ford was unbelievably competitive and relatively inexpensive back in the mid-70s.

At Brands Hatch, for example, you'd usually have an entry list of 72 drivers, divided into three heats of 24, with the top eight in each heat going through to the final. The racing was tremendously close, with so much overtaking that it was difficult for spectators to know where to look next. There were accidents galore, most of which were quite harmless, and the public loved it. So many of the drivers with whom I was competing almost every week at that time went on to bigger and better things: Derek Warwick, Derek Daly, James Weaver, Chico Serra, Eddie Cheever and the most famous of all, Nigel Mansell, are just a few of the Formula Ford pack of that era who moved into Formula 1 or top flight international motor racing.

I still find it surprising today, some 30 years on, just how many of the drivers who I got to know well in those heady days of Formula Ford racing, are still in the motorsport business. Many of these have become good friends of mine.

John Webb, managing director of Brands Hatch, was the man who made that famous circuit really buzz in those days. One of his brilliant ideas was to stage an annual BBC Radio 1 Fun Day at the track. It used to be packed out with people, many of whom only came to meet the pop stars of the era and listen to the music, but it didn't matter. Brands Hatch was the place to be and racing in front of those huge crowds was quite an experience. I recall a very young Noel Edmonds racing in a celebrity race in a Ford Escort Mexico and doing so well that he progressed to a semi-professional racing career for a while. Webb also brought some famous sportswomen into motor racing and I raced against the captain of the British ski team, Davina Galica, on many an occasion. The Olympic show jumper, Ann Moore, was another who came into motor racing thanks to the efforts of John Webb. It was no wonder that he was able to secure sponsorship for the race meetings at his circuit. He came up with good value, innovative concepts that might have upset many of the purists, but drew the crowds in.

It was at one of these Radio 1 Fun Days that my dreams of glamour truly came to the fore.

The meeting included a round of the national Formula Ford Championship in which I was competing. I recall that it was Webb's intention to have three pop celebrities present the awards on the podium after the race to the first three drivers in the race.

I remember that Olivia Newton-John was there, as was Babs from Pan's People, the resident dance group on Top of the Pops. My favourite singer at that time was also there, Lynsey De Paul, who was to eventually marry James Coburn, the film star.

Mainly because of a first corner pile-up, I was fortunate enough to find myself in third place on that podium and desperately hoped that it would be Lynsey De Paul who would present me with a trophy.

Up stepped Olivia to kiss the winner, then the second placed driver received his Cup from Babs of Pan's People. Yes, I thought, it's going to be Lynsey! That's when the glamour temporarily went out of motor racing for me – instead of Lynsey De Paul, up stepped a whopping eight-foot-tall Uncle Bulgaria of the Wombles to shake my hand! It transpired that their record, Remember I'm A Womble, had just moved into the top ten and they were big stars at the time.

"My sponsors revelled in the huge crowds and atmosphere of the Radio 1 day – something that conventional advertising can't deliver"

Of course, my sponsors at that time just revelled in the huge crowds and atmosphere of the Radio 1 day and that is something that conventional advertising can't deliver, the opportunity for a company to get so close to their potential customers. My major sponsor had brought most of their sales force along for a day, together with spouses, friends and family. A great time was had by all. The result was a highly motivated bunch of salespeople, all wanting to do well and to earn the right to be invited to a subsequent track day which the company had introduced as a sales incentive prize. This would entail the salespeople actually driving racing cars, under supervision, at the same track where they had watched me race.

That brings us nicely back to the business of finding sponsors. We've looked at the way in which you start your sales strategy by creating a sponsorship opportunity that is relevant to companies, in other words a product that is saleable. You've also seen the importance of putting a realistic valuation on your sponsorship property.

When you put your list together, as I described in the last chapter, you should be able to come up with a number of features that your sponsorship property is capable of delivering. Before moving onto the next step in the strategy, I want to spend some time looking at an area which involves these features and in which I find a lot of people make some fundamental errors.

I can put my hand on my heart and state that this is an aspect of selling that everyone thinks they understand, but which in practice, the majority of sponsorship-seekers seem to forget. It concerns the difference between what constitutes a feature or entitlement of a sponsorship property, what constitutes an advantage, and finally, what constitutes a benefit. Now I know that there will be many of you immediately flicking through the pages to the next section, thinking that this is old hat. I can

Brian joined Olympic Silver Medallist show jumper, Anne Moore, as a judge in a national beauty contest staged by his Formula Ford Sponsor ITT FOCUS

understand you thinking that, but my response to that is, if it is so simple, why do so many people still get it wrong? If understanding the difference between features, advantages and benefits is so important, I should start by defining what they are, in relation to your sponsorship opportunity.

A feature is a fact or characteristic of your sponsorship property. No more than that. An advantage illustrates how the right feature might be able to satisfy a marketing need of the prospect. A benefit illustrates how the right feature and its advantage specifically meets that prospect's identified need, as confirmed by the prospect.

I should add that it is not only in sponsorship that this applies. Imagine that you are trying to sell your car to a prospective buyer. You've identified a number of features that you want to bring to their attention.

Let's take one as an example:
– A **feature** might be the soft top which can be folded back.
– An **advantage** of this **feature** might be that you can fold it back and enjoy sitting in the sun.
– Is this **advantage** the same as a **benefit**? Not necessarily. It transpires that your potential buyer lives in a particularly rough part of town. The thought of having a soft top which can easily be slashed open is not going to be at all beneficial. But your next caller for the car lives by the coast and is young enough to want to impress girlfriends and likes to create a sporty image. To this person, the soft top is particularly beneficial. This time the **advantage** is a **benefit**. This is the point that I want to stress. The **feature** hasn't changed, neither has the potential **advantage**. The only thing that has changed is the fact that what is a **benefit** to one person might well be a negative to another.

It's the same with sponsorship. Take this example of a **feature** (or entitlement) offered by a Formula 1 team to a potential sponsor:
– The **feature** is the provision of six advertising boards trackside at each Grand Prix.
– The **advantage** is the estimated 350 million people will see the sponsor's company name or brand.
– Is this a **benefit**? Not necessarily. The first prospect is a company that offers high-fee financial consultancy to major blue-chip corporations. Its need for name awareness is extremely limited and

would not be worth the cost involved. Hospitality and case study development might be the features that excite this company. This **feature** is not a **benefit** to them. However, the next prospect is a mobile phone service provider who has changed brand name and is looking to create awareness on a large scale. This **feature** could be an extremely important **benefit** to this company

Therefore:
– **Features** of your sponsorship property are factual and don't change.
– **Advantages** that those **features** can offer don't change, varied as they may be.
– **Benefits** exist only if the **feature** is an **advantage** to the company to whom you are presenting. If it isn't, then that **feature** is not a **benefit**.

The successful presentation of your sponsorship opportunity can be analysed as identifying the entitlements (**features**) that are an **advantage** to the company in question and which will provide them with a **benefit**, as confirmed by them.

Example:
– **Feature**: 20 day's use of a replica full-size display car.
– **Advantage**: This can provide an attention-grabbing display at a show.
– **Benefit**: The company to whom you are talking, are exhibiting at the Ideal Home Exhibition and a display car would allow it to offer visitors to the exhibition the opportunity to have their photographs taken sitting in the display car, after which they can sample the company's new confectionery brand.

Prior to a meaningful discussion with that prospect, the entitlement of being able to use a display car is only a feature of your sponsorship property. Yes, its advantage is the opportunity to use it as a crowd-puller, but it's only if the company believe that it will work for them that it becomes a benefit.

If you present your sponsorship opportunities in terms of benefits, you will increase your success rate quite dramatically. You can only do this by asking the right questions, listening to the answers and then selecting only those features that are most likely to offer a benefit to that specific company.

I strongly believe that a lot of time can be wasted trying to flog the proverbial dead horse, when the fact of the matter is that you should be honest enough to know when what you have to offer simply doesn't in any way meet the needs of your prospect. If you genuinely don't believe that your sponsorship opportunity is capable of delivering what the prospect is looking for, be honest enough to admit that. Don't confuse persistence with stubbornness.

If you think that you can help the prospect, persistence is a valuable quality. If you know in your heart that you can't help, but you don't want to accept the fact, that is stubbornness.

SUMMARY

It is important to fully understand the difference between features, advantages and benefits. Features of your sponsorship property are essentially facts. Advantages demonstrate how those facts might become a benefit. Benefits are only derived when the potential sponsor confirms that the features and advantages suit its specific needs.

It is important to remember that what is a benefit to one company, might be a disadvantage to another. If you present features and advantages and then ask questions to determine if these are potential benefits, you'll face far fewer objections than if you try to present everything as a benefit.

Until your prospect confirms which of the features are beneficial, they are never anything other than features. The more benefits that you identify, the greater your chance of securing a sponsorship deal.

A **multi-dimensional** approach

The next logical step in the strategy development would be to identify the companies that you want to approach. However, before we set about that – which we all know isn't an easy thing to achieve – there is an important aspect of sponsorship seeking which I want to introduce you to. It's not a magic formula; I've already told you that there is no such thing. What I want to look at is a different approach to the way that you go about marketing your sponsorship opportunity to add greater value to it.

Instead of simply sitting down at the computer and creating a list of companies that you feel could be potential sponsors, I want to show you another option. If I had to put a name to it I think I would call it "multi-dimensional planning". It has been a method that I have used for many years and one that has helped me to secure some extremely worthwhile sponsorship deals at all levels, from a few thousand up to a few million pounds.

Perhaps some of you are already familiar with it, but even if you are, please don't ignore this chapter. It can play such a vital role in the successful negotiation of a meaningful sponsorship programme that I don't think you are wasting your time going through it again. If it is new to you, I want to assure you that it is well worth making sure you fully understand its implications before moving on.

Multi-dimensional planning means that instead of targeting companies one by one, you devise various strategies that allow you to link together a number of companies that can potentially each benefit from the involvement of the others. It can incorporate the increasingly popular practice of business-to-business marketing, but this is not the only multi-dimensional strategy, as you will see.

I think that the most effective way of explaining what I mean when I talk about multi-dimensional planning is to use some examples to demonstrate the technique.

Back in the real heyday of American IndyCar racing, a sponsorship deal was constructed which was so successful that it stayed in place for more than ten years. The deal involved a well-known company in the States called K-Mart. At that time, there were K-Mart stores in just about every town, selling a range of products from baby apparel to home electronics, from food to car oil. The leading team in the IndyCar Championship was then Newman-Haas Racing, for whom the Andrettis drove, both father and son. Hollywood star Paul Newman was a partner in the team and one of the most natural people you could hope to meet. In later years, Nigel Mansell went over to America and won the IndyCar Championship at his first attempt, driving for the Newman-Haas team.

The sponsorship deal to which I refer was brokered by a colleague of mine in the States on behalf of Newman-Haas Racing. The first part of the deal was fairly standard:
- K-Mart would become the Title Sponsor of the Newman-Haas team
- They would be given a large allocated amount of space on the cars and drivers' suits
- There would be K-Mart branding on the sides of the car and on the rear wing
- There would still be spaces left over which K-Mart had been allocated but not used
- The team's cars and drivers would be made available to K-Mart on a promotional basis in selected stores when there was a nearby IndyCar race. This would be publicised by K-Mart in the local press, guaranteeing a large turn-out of people at the store to meet the drivers, see the cars and get autographs
- K-Mart would be able to use images of the team and drivers in its advertising.

"For them to have continued for ten years shows that it must have been well worth their while in respect of a business return"

Now comes the innovative part. There would obviously be a significant sponsorship fee involved. K-Mart approached several key suppliers and proposed that these suppliers should also become sponsors of the team, paying K-Mart a sponsorship fee. In return for agreeing to this, they would receive a number of entitlements:
- Branding on the cars in the spaces still owned, but not used, by K-Mart
- Prime merchandising opportunities in-store
- Participation in K-Mart exclusive promotions and mail drops
- The right to promotional activities when the team cars and drivers were in-store
- Participation in exclusive K-Mart adverting activities based on the sponsorship of the team
- Several other entitlements, which were added to these main points.

In this way, K-Mart effectively enjoyed a major sponsorship programme of one of the sport's most high-profile and successful motor racing teams, with virtually all of the sponsorship fee being paid for by several of their key suppliers. Companies that took up this unique opportunity included Gillette, Dirt Devil, Havoline and Energiser. For them to have continued for ten years shows that it must have been well worth their while in respect of a business return.

This is just one example of what I call multi-dimensional planning. Had the broker simply approached K-Mart with a straightforward sponsorship deal, not involving any other companies, there may have been some interest, but it would have been a hard sell. However, by approaching them with this strategic alliance concept, he was able to show them all of the benefits that could be derived, together with a highly effective way of recouping their sponsorship fee. It really was a win-win situation, because everyone involved benefited. The suppliers were happy because it gave them all the normal benefits of a sponsorship programme, but in addition, it secured for them an exclusive relationship with one of their biggest customers.

Another example of multi-dimensional planning, one that approaches the task of securing sponsorship from a different angle, is Bath Rugby Club. Once the top amateur club, Bath now plays in the highly professional Zurich Premiership and is sponsored by a famous cider brand, Blackthorn.

The Blackthorn brand is owned by the Matthew Clark Group. Within the Zurich Premiership regulations, a team is allowed to display three sponsor's brand identities on the players' shirts. In 2000, Bath only had Blackthorn, the club's title sponsor, on its team shirt and I was given the task of securing two additional new sponsorship deals.

Instead of approaching a random number of companies that might be interested in becoming a sponsor, I used multi-dimensional planning to focus my approach. What I set out to do was to create a strategy that would provide the three sponsors and Bath with a way of doing potential business together in addition to the benefits that each sponsor would normally expect to generate.

I decided to approach companies from business sectors that firstly might benefit from an association with Blackthorn and, secondly, that could provide valuable expertise to Bath as a business. The two business categories that I identified as offering the greatest potential for this were IT and mobile communications. This immediately made the task of targeting companies a lot easier.

Having set out what I wanted to achieve, my next step was an important part of the multi-dimensional plan. During that year, I had developed a good relationship with the Blackthorn brand managing director, Rob MacNevin. Prior to joining Blackthorn, Rob held a senior marketing position within Guinness and had been involved in putting together the Kaliber sponsorship deal of the Ford team in the British Touring Car Championship. He really understood how sponsorship worked for a company and so I put forward a proposal as to how he could help me bring in another two sponsors.

It was in Blackthorn's interest that we secured two appropriate sponsors. They would not be keen on an association with companies with the "wrong" image. This is an important point to remember; if you secure a sponsorship deal with a major brand, it will not be appreciated if you then announce to them that you have also secured a sponsorship agreement with a local kebab shop (no disrespect to kebabs!)

I arranged a meeting with Rob MacNevin to communicate to him that I wanted to introduce an IT partner to Bath. I went on to explain that in addition to a sponsorship fee, an IT partner could equip the club with urgently required IT hardware and also provide the expertise to set up such processes as online ticketing, computerised stock control in the club's retail shop and so on. He was happy to hear this, as it would enhance the potential for Blackthorn to further promote its brand.

I then asked him if he would make it possible for me to offer a very important entitlement to those potential IT and mobile communication sponsors I identified: the potential to do business with the Matthew Clark Group. The company spent a considerable amount on its IT infrastructure, including a call centre. I was not seeking an assurance that they would do business with a company that I introduced to them. There is no way that any major company would entertain that notion. All that I wanted the Blackthorn MD to agree to was for me to be able to guarantee to an IT company that if it became a sponsor of Bath, I would arrange a meeting for that company with the purchasing director of Matthew Clark. No more than that. It would then be up to the IT company's sales personnel to conduct a normal presentation of their product range. Whether or not they eventually secured business would be down to their own sales skills and Matthew Clark's discretion. In a similar way, I wanted to provide the mobile communications company with the same opportunity.

Rob saw no problem with this and even introduced me to the purchasing director to make sure that he was in agreement. This helped me initially to secure a major sponsorship deal for Bath with a leading IT company, Northgate Information Systems, who became the club's official IT partner. As part of the sponsorship agreement, Northgate conducted an IT audit at Bath and subsequently designed and supplied a new IT infrastructure for the club.

As it turned out, the second deal was with a mobile phone company. Again, the potential business opportunities that were presented were attractive, but it was the opportunity to market phones through the Bath retail shop in the centre of Bath that was particularly innovative. The community involvement aspect was also a major consideration for this company, Virgin Mobile.

There was another reason that I was keen to secure Virgin Mobile as a sponsor for Bath. The average age of Bath's supporters at that time was quite high and it was apparent that the club needed to attract more youngsters. I knew that the Virgin Mobile brand appealed more to a younger audience than other mobile phone companies. I also knew that Virgin Mobile would be a very pro-active sponsor, which is just what was needed. I remember the shock waves amongst some of the more elderly and staid members of Bath when the first Virgin Mobile advertisement appeared in the official programme. It showed the face of a very attractive young woman, sticking her tongue out rather suggestively. "Virgin Mobile, sponsors of Bath Rugby.....lick 'em boys!" read the caption.

The sponsorship has proved a huge success and it has certainly succeeded in attracting the interest of many more young people to Bath.

One of the first things I did when I had signed these two deals, was to invite the CEO's of all three companies, Blackthorn, Northgate and Virgin Mobile, to lunch so they could meet each other and explore ways in which they might be able to do business together, using Bath as the catalyst.

These are just a couple of examples of how you can create a multi-dimensional plan to approach the task of finding sponsors. By looking for ways to create a possible alliance between companies, using the sponsorship programme as a means to do so, you are able to add considerable extra value to the proposals. It's important to remember, however, that although this method can add value to the sponsorship opportunity, you will still need to build a very strong case for sponsorship in the normal way for each company that you approach.

The two examples that I have used are by no means the only way of using this method. You need to be creative, but you will soon get used to thinking in this way. Take these three categories of business, and see if you can create a way of bringing them together around a sponsorship opportunity:
• Business equipment distributor
• Office furniture supplier
• Insurance company.

I want you to work this out for yourselves, but let me point you in the right direction. A business equipment distributor: employs salespeople; owns several company cars; has a large office and showroom; has a potential need for insurance; has a potential need for office furniture.

Now do the same for the other two and you'll be able to put together a possible strategy for creating an interesting potential alliance. Thinking about the situation in this way and it becomes relatively easy to apply any of these examples, and your own ideas, to your particular sponsorship opportunity. The principle can be applied to any situation; The K-Mart example could work just as well for your local hardware store and some of its suppliers.

One of the most important benefits that I have derived from using this system is that it helps me identify which companies I should be approaching. In the next chapter I want to expand on the subject of multi-dimensional planning and look at other ways in which sponsorship deals can be constructed.

SUMMARY

If you devise strategic sales plans, which use your sponsorship property as a catalyst for business development, it can help you identify which companies might offer a higher level of potential.

Strategic sales plans need to be creative and practical. If you can involve a group of companies, it will increase the value of the sponsorship opportunity for those involved. Companies will be more receptive to sponsorship opportunities that demonstrate how they might improve their bottom line; bringing like-minded companies to help develop new business opportunities should gain their interest.

Chaucer Group

About the Chaucer Group

An award winning, independent management consultancy that supports clients in six main practise areas:

- Project and programme management
- Information technology*
- Mergers, acquisitions and joint ventures
- Human resources
- Supply chain
- Sales and marketing.

The company's reputation is based upon its capability to successfully deliver business change projects to a wide range of clients from different industry sectors. Chaucer Group has been successfully trading since 1987, providing high-quality management and information technology services to industry and commerce worldwide. The group brings together high quality management with leading digital know-how to create a unique offering.

Chaucer Group is a UK company with headquarters in Canterbury, Kent, and operational offices in North America, the Middle East and the Far East. It trades as Chaucer Consulting and Chaucer Digital on a global basis.

Case Study

This case study provides an excellent example of the way a relatively small sponsorship programme can grow into a much larger involvement, provided that there is a healthy ongoing relationship between the two parties involved.

For the past three years, Chaucer Group has been involved in small, but cost-effective, commercial relationships with the famous Wolverhampton Wanderers Football Club, better known as Wolves, who currently play in the Coca Cola Championship (formerly known as the First Division). The involvement has included match ball and official programme sponsorships, as well as the use of considerable corporate hospitality.

The nature of the business in which Chaucer is involved means that it is precluded from advertising or promoting the name of its clients. The global organisations and other high profile businesses for which Chaucer works demand a high degree of confidentiality. The majority of Chaucer's clients are initially introduced by referrals and so the subsequent client-relationship management is an essential part of business development for Chaucer.

* Including IT strategy, software development, systems implementation and application hosting, all through Chaucer Digital.

Historically, Chaucer has used corporate hospitality to effectively develop and maintain client relationships. Football, with its broad level of attraction, both nationally and internationally, has always been high on the list of hospitality events and Chaucer had previously taken clients to several different Premiership football clubs as well as Wolves. Of these, it was found that Wolverhampton Wanderers was the most friendly and accommodating club in terms of meeting the specific requirements of Chaucer and hence its clients. Feedback from guests indicated that the access to management and players, together with the format used, made their visit very memorable, extremely enjoyable and rather special.

Based on this feedback, Chaucer decided to increase their use of Wolves' hospitality for the entertainment of clients and prospective clients. In addition, they entered into an agreement that would provide the company with a small amount of branding on the interview-area backdrop. On one occasion, after a match against Chelsea at Molineux, an interview with Chelsea manager Claudio Ranieri was broadcast on TV. Throughout the interview, which lasted for several minutes, the Chaucer logo seemingly perched on the tip of his nose. This resulted in e-mails and faxes being received from all over the world, from existing clients and other companies Chaucer had been in contact with. It generated conversations with a lot of key people and was therefore seen as having worked well.

For the Chaucer Chairman, Bob Laslett, and his team, this highlighted the potential that increased brand awareness could offer the company. Although it would never play as important a role in the marketing plan as it might do for a fast-moving consumer goods type of business, it could still contribute significantly. Creating brand awareness for a management consultancy is never easy, but after seeing the positive results that were being achieved from the association with Wolves, it was decided to investigate the feasibility of a further increase in the relationship with the club. It was felt that such an increase could also be helpful in providing the company's own staff with a more visible focus.

For a company the size of Chaucer, this type of marketing has to be used in a very prudent manner. Unless a clear commercial return could be shown, an increase in the use of sports sponsorship could not be justified. In considering the growth of their sponsorship activities, consideration was given to the feedback from Chaucer guests at previous hospitality events at Molineux. On the occasions when the company had sponsored the match ball, two guests were normally given the opportunity to go onto the pitch in front of 29,000 fans. This proved very popular. An increased level of sponsorship would provide a far greater opportunity for guest participation and was therefore deemed to be important. It made the guest feel special and tended to further consolidate the relationship between Chaucer and its guests.

Chaucer was also aware that client hospitality has to be undertaken in a responsible and professional manner and should be both enjoyable and a learning experience. It realised that football has the added benefit of being played at the weekend or in the evening and therefore doesn't impact on the normal working day as many other forms of hospitality can do.

Although the continued use of hospitality as a stand-alone marketing tool could achieve good results, it was decided that a more in-depth sponsorship would warrant the additional expense by providing a closer link between the company and its guests. The increase in brand awareness would be welcome, particularly on TV, with English football now being broadcast by TV channels all over the world.

Another important consideration in the decision to increase the company's involvement with Wolves was the perception, or image transfer, that would be generated. Chaucer perceived several key qualities and values associated with Wolves as important and beneficial, if applied to themselves. These included:
• A reputation for sound commercial management
• Prudence
• Financial stability
• An illustrious history
• A very powerful brand
• A friendly persona
• Traditional values
• Passion for the product
• Open and honest management.

The sponsorship
The decision by Chaucer to become the major sponsor at the Club was based on several major business principles:
• Brand awareness
• Hospitality
• Image transfer
• Participation
• Case study development.

From the start of the 2004/5 season, Chaucer have been the official club sponsor of Wolverhampton Wanderers. This means that their brand appears prominently across the front of the team shirts, as well as on all replica kit. A range of other branding opportunities is incorporated, which includes signage and advertising. The sponsorship package, not surprisingly, provides extensive hospitality opportunities.

In addition to being the club sponsor, Chaucer provide Wolverhampton Wanderers with an agreed level of management consultancy, helping the club further develop its business expertise. In return, Chaucer will be able to develop a case study on how it was able to work closely with such a high-profile entity as Wolves to manage many aspects of business management. This will be helpful when presenting to potential new clients.

Having played the previous season in the Premiership, the question was discussed as to whether the club's relegation would have any impact on Chaucer decision to become the club sponsor. The unanimous verdict was that it would not have any negative effect. The benefits that would accrue from the association with Wolves would apply equally, whether the team was in the Premiership or in the new Coca Cola Championship. It was also felt that as the sponsorship of the Football League has been taken over by Coca Cola, the amount of promotion that would be provided by such a high profile, proactive global company could only benefit the team and Chaucer Consulting.

Measurement

As a management consultancy, Chaucer is focused on business performance for major global enterprises. The company is constantly involved in the measurement of improved performance through "change" projects. The identification of key performance indicators is a core part of its business activity.

The company has put in place a set of these key performance indicators to measure its sponsorship of Wolves. It is very important that the sponsorship can be constantly measured in a tangible way to ensure that it delivers all that it promised.

These indicators include measurement of direct contact that is made by clients and potential clients with the company's sponsorship. They also include the measurement of business-to-business opportunities with other sponsors, advertisers and commercial contacts of Wolverhampton Wanderers.

Here is an example of how the measurement process is already tracking contacts that are being made:

The Chaucer office received a call at the time that the Wolves sponsorship deal had just been announced. It came from a senior manager of a company that had no current relationship with Chaucer, but that Chaucer would very much like to do business with. He had seen the announcement of the Wolves sponsorship and it had caused him to remember that he had worked with Bob Laslett nearly 20 years ago.

His call was put through to the Chaucer Chairman and the pair had an interesting conversation, during which the caller informed him that he had been a Wolves season ticket holder for many years. This eventually led Bob Laslett to mention that he would very much appreciate an introduction to a couple of key people within the company for which the caller worked. The response was positive and it was agreed that an attempt would be made to secure a meeting with these people.

This business opportunity came about through the announcement of Chaucer being the new Wolves sponsor. As such, this would now be entered into the measurement process.

Some of the key performance indicators are factually driven, such as the business that is directly generated. Others are less factual and more concerned with the measurement of perceptions, relationship management and business introductions.

Author's comments

This case study shows that through the careful management and nurturing of a sponsor, however small, in the early days, there is the potential for that company to eventually grow into a major sponsor.

Chaucer has entered into this major sponsorship agreement with its eyes wide open. Although the enthusiasm of the chairman is a driving force in its progression, the decision to move forward has been made on purely commercial grounds and a stringent set of measurement criteria have been put in place.

Brand awareness has been a key factor, but the use of hospitality, the development of business-to-business opportunities and the association with the perceived qualities of Wolves have also been major considerations. In addition, the opportunity for Chaucer to develop a powerful case study has added even further value to the agreed programme.

The power of **the media**

I mentioned at the beginning of this book that there is no magic formula that I can disclose to you that will make you more successful in securing sponsorship. I wish there was such a thing. However, although it's not a formula, there are common threads that run through many of the sponsorship deals that I have put together over the years. In the last chapter, I outlined the system of multi-dimensional planning that I use a great deal. I also mentioned that I would disclose some other ways of applying this method and that is what I want to do now.

One of the many of the reasons that companies use sponsorship is to be able to generate a higher and more effective level of media coverage than relying purely on conventional paid-for advertising. All companies like positive media coverage and are always looking for cost-effective ways of generating it. The problem with many sponsorship proposals is that they refer blandly to the fact that their sport/championship/team generates a high amount of media coverage and leave it at that. While true, it is fairly meaningless. What if you could state that in the next 12 months there are going to be three TV programmes that will feature you or your sports activity, as well as two major features in a Sunday newspaper? Would that not add considerable value to your proposal?

The problem is that media coverage doesn't work that way. You're probably already thinking that unless you're Tim Henman, playing at Wimbledon, or Arsenal playing in Europe, you won't get any substantial guaranteed media coverage. You're right. Under normal circumstances you can't guarantee this. However, what I very often do when designing a sponsorship sales strategy is to find a way of making it happen. If you can build in a high level of guaranteed powerful media coverage, you have a head start over many of your rivals when you are looking for a share of that sponsorship cake.

There are several ways of going about this task, but I want to look at two specific strategies that I use a great deal of the time and can honestly say that they work more often than not. I think that the best way to demonstrate how I use this method is to look at a brief case study of a deal that I put together in South Africa.

Example 1

In the late 1980s, Group C Sportscar racing was at its peak. These were basically the cars that raced in the top class at the world famous Le Mans 24-hours race. The World Championship was extremely well supported and included many famous teams.

Amongst the most high profile of these were the Rothman Porsches, driven by Jochen Mass, Stefan Bellof, Jackie Ickx and Derek Bell. These cars were capable of speeds well over 220 mph.

Traditionally, at the end of the season, the teams would compete in an endurance race at the Kyalami Grand Prix circuit in South Africa. It was normal for a few of the international teams to select a South African driver to join their normal driver line-up. In most cases, this still meant that the driver would be required to bring along sponsorship for the team. In how many sports does that happen?

In 1987, I was driving for the Honda touring car team in South Africa and relished the idea of competing in this televised international race at the end of the season, the Yellow Pages 500. As it happened, that year there were two races on two successive weekends. I was invited by one of the overseas teams to drive for them in both events and set about securing the fairly substantial amount of sponsorship that I would need. I had exactly six weeks to find an amount, which today would equate to around £75,000. It was a lot of money to find in a short time. I knew that I would have to be very creative in coming up with an attractive strategy. This is how I set about the task.

"When they learned that I wasn't looking for sponsorship money from them, they took a little more notice than at first"

First of all, I contacted The Sunday Times newspaper, South Africa's largest circulation paper. I explained that this prestigious international race was coming to South Africa and went on to suggest that the readers of the paper might find it interesting to learn how the business of sponsorship in motor racing worked. My own search for sponsorship would provide a good example. When they learned that I wasn't looking for sponsorship money from them, neither was I expecting them to write a feature about my performance in the race, they took a little more notice than at first.

What I proposed was that I would write a feature article for them about the business of sponsorship-hunting in motor racing. In return, I would not expect a fee. What I asked for was that they would guarantee a three-page feature and that they would include a large colour photograph of the racing car, carrying the livery of whichever sponsor that I was able to secure. After quite a lot of discussions about this, they eventually came back to me and confirmed that they liked the idea. A deal was struck. The problem was that I still had no money and had to find the sponsor, otherwise I would have nothing to write about.

I then doubled the problem by offering a similar opportunity to another publication. This time it was South Africa's top-selling lifestyle magazine, Style, a high-quality glossy, full-colour monthly magazine which covered all the glitzy social activities within the Transvaal. I convinced them that although it was a motor race and they didn't cover sport, it was going to be a big social occasion with lots of personalities and glamour. This time I suggested that they had their branding on the car, in return for a major feature on the lifestyle of a professional racing driver, namely me. They liked the idea and after I had checked with both publications that there would be no conflict of interest, we agreed a deal. Style then dispatched a reporter to have a poolside breakfast at my house with both my wife and myself, to find out all sort of things about my lifestyle as a racing driver.

I was now getting nervous, as I still hadn't approached a single potential fee-paying sponsor. I knew that sticking to my strategy was my only chance of putting this together.

My next step was to make contact with SABC, the South African equivalent of the BBC and spoke to the producer of a programme called Graffiti, a programme not unlike Richard and Judy, with guests from various walks of life. I explained to the producer that I felt it might be interesting for the viewers to discover the ways in which a driver, who is not a big name star, has to secure a drive in this much heralded international race that was taking place in South Africa. She liked my idea and arranged a date for me to go onto the programme.

I now realised I was going to have some pretty serious egg on my face if I couldn't deliver a sponsorship. I had three extremely high-profile media organisations build me into their schedules and I still didn't even have a penny to pay for the drive that I had been offered.

It was time to get on the phone and start contacting companies in search of that £75,000. It took me no fewer than 60 calls before I eventually hit the jackpot. Based on the guaranteed high level of media exposure that I was able to offer, in addition to all the other entitlements that came with it, I was able to conclude a deal. It was not quite what I had expected but at least enabled me to secure the drive.

The company in question was called GBS Wang, the Wang computer distributors for South Africa. I had managed to arrange a meeting with the chairman of the company who, fortunately for me, had the vision to see the potential for his company and was able to make a fast decision. GBS Wang agreed to about 60 per cent of the total that I required, but were happy for me to secure a another sponsor for the second weekend's race. This meant I had to go back to the phone. A few more calls were made and I found the required sponsor for the second weekend. This time it was a South African retail jewellery chain called Sterns. With just ten days to go I had managed to put not one, but two, sponsorship deals together. It had been touch and go, but I had the confidence that my strategy would pay dividends. As I said at the beginning of this book, confidence breeds success.

The main reason I'd been successful was that I had put together a programme of guaranteed media activities that made the deal attractive. I had stressed to both sponsors that this media coverage negated the very real risk that exists in motor racing, that I could crash out on the first lap of both events. What I had promised them, not literally, was that they would have had full value for money by 6pm on the evening before the race. Whatever happened on race day was a bonus, the icing on the cake.

As for the media coverage, it was better than I could have expected. The Sunday Times article, called "Executive Behind the Wheel" appeared over three pages in the centre of its colour supplement magazine. A sideways view of the racing car, resplendent in GBS branding, was spread across the front two pages. On the third page, a smaller, but effective photo of the car in Sterns livery appeared. I was also able to explain why both companies became involved in the events in the feature that I wrote.

Style magazine approached it from a totally different angle, including a photo of the GBS chairman sitting in the car. This appeared in the magazine's society pages, in which everyone normally stands with a glass of champagne in their hands, smiling uneasily. In addition, the three-page feature, which had the title "Wanna Race My Car, Babe!" was humorous. Totally inaccurate, but very effective.

The TV programme went well and I was able to talk about both sponsorships in some detail during my five-minute interview, outlining how I had put the deals together.

Finally, the race itself went to plan. There was considerable TV coverage of the car, the corporate entertaining proved to be very successful and it proved to be a win-win situation for each of the parties involved – providing another example of successful multi-dimensional planning. It demonstrated that by developing a strategy that secures a guaranteed level of media coverage, there is far more likelihood of generating interest when you make your initial sales approach to a potential sponsor. It will also help you in your targeting of companies. By knowing the markets that the media sources appeal to, you can direct your sales efforts towards companies that have similar target markets.

Example 2

Another sales strategy that involves the use of the media is often referred to as a media barter deal. This is rather more simplistic, but can be quite effective. It involves the approach to a media source, such as a commercial radio station or regional newspaper, although it can apply to any media source that carries commercial advertising. It starts with an approach to the media organisation in the same way that you would go about presenting a sponsorship proposal to any prospective company. The difference is that when, as so often happens, the media organisation informs you that they don't have a budget for conventional sports sponsorship, you offer them an alternative way of funding the programme. What you propose is that in return for a certain amount of branding and/or other sponsorship entitlements, they provide you with the following: an agreed amount of advertising space or airtime, which you can either sell on, or use for your own purposes; a guaranteed number of feature articles or programmes relating to your sponsorship property.

If they accept the proposal, what have you actually achieved? For a start, you have some guaranteed media coverage in place. Secondly, you have an amount of advertising space or airtime that has a specific value and which you can use to your advantage. What I would normally do with

"Don't give away a silly amount of entitlements to the media sponsor, and make sure you can afford to allocate them an area of branding"

this is to immediately include that space in a sponsorship proposal to a company that you might expect to consider the publication or radio station important. This will add value to your sponsorship proposal and help you justify your fee to the prospective sponsor.

This is how it works. Assume that you have a sponsorship proposal that you would normally value at £50,000. Thanks to your media sponsorship deal, you now have an amount of advertising space that is valued at £20,000 (being calculated at the lowest rate available to a major advertiser). You can now include that space in your proposal. It would make sense to now increase that sponsorship fee, but not by the full value of the media space. You instead decide to add only 25 per cent of the true value of that space, making your sponsorship fee £55,000. That represents good value for the potential sponsor, assuming that your original valuation was correct. The sponsor is now being offered £20,000 worth of advertising for only £5,000 and this is in addition to all of the other entitlements that the sponsorship brings them, as well as the benefit of guaranteed media features that you secured as part of your agreement.

From your point of view, it's a good deal, provided that you didn't give away a silly amount of entitlements to the media sponsor and that you can afford to allocate them an area of branding. This should normally be an area which you would not expect to sell anyway. What you have succeeded in doing is to bring on board a new sponsor, a new media partner and have gained £5,000 in the process.

SUMMARY

The use of the media as a powerful sales tool is very effective. By offering a guaranteed level of media coverage to potential sponsors, in addition to that which would normally be expected within the sponsorship programme, you are adding meaningful extra value. You need to plan this carefully and prove that the media partners you bring on board will appeal to the companies you then approach.

There are two ways of working with the media in this way. One is to secure media partners, using the guaranteed features to attract other sponsors. The other way is to enter into media barter deals. These provide you with a guaranteed level of media advertising space or airtime, which you can use within a sponsorship proposal to increase its value. It may be possible to also include a small level of feature coverage into these barter deals as well.

Chapter 9

Where do you **start?**

I'm not sure how many registered companies there are in the UK, but I believe it is in excess of 1.6 million. Add in all the smaller, non-incorporated businesses and you have a market that can surely provide you with at least one sponsor (a mere 0.0000625 per cent of the companies that you can theoretically contact). Once you've found your sponsor and secured your budget, you can get on with the business of doing well in your particular sport.

Of course, we all know that life doesn't work like that. Deciding which companies to contact is one of the most difficult parts of the sponsorship-seeking process. With so many out there, you're spoilt for choice. It's rather like a child being let loose in a chocolate factory and told they can choose any bar they like, but only one!

You might be thinking that instead of talking about which companies to contact, the next logical step in the marketing strategy should be the creation of a sponsorship presentation. A lot of people do just that at this stage in the sales strategy and it's not for me to say this is wrong. But I feel that there is an advantage to be had in holding back on this, until you've finalised the plans that will determine which companies you approach. By doing so, you'll have a far better idea of the companies that you are going to target and will be able to design a modular presentation that you can "mix and match" to suit the industry sector they are in. As a result, it will be more effective. So I'm asking you to bear with me on this and leave the design of a presentation until later in the process.

There are two main ways of targeting these companies.

The first is the shotgun approach. What this means is that you compile a large list of businesses from, say, a local trade directory or a database service. You then contact as many as you can, on the basis that, according to the law of averages, one will be interested.

This is an extremely common approach and it obviously works for some people. The problem is that it rules out any meaningful research on the companies being carried out before you make contact. The time needed to do this would be considerable and, in most cases, prohibitive. This approach comes down largely to luck; whether you just happen to hit the right company at the right time on the right person's desk.

It also makes meaningful follow-up almost impossible. For follow-up to be effective it should be done within 2-3 days of the proposal or communication being sent. If you send out a large number, at virtually the same time, there is little chance of you having the time to do this properly.

The other option is to adopt what is best described as the rifle approach. This is the careful identification of companies that match certain criteria that you have set out, prior to making contact. It usually involves being in contact with no more than a dozen companies at a time. In this way, you will be able to research the companies, and follow them up in a meaningful manner. It will also allow you to follow up each contact within the desired period of time.

I would never totally rule out the shotgun approach. It's feasible to perhaps send out a mailshot, offering a specific sponsorship opportunity to a known database. It might be, for example, that a sports venue is seeking a small amount of sponsorship for a forthcoming event. To mail all the venue's existing advertisers, corporate hospitality clients and local business contacts could well make sense.

"The first thing to do when devising your targeting strategy is to establish an initial selection criteria"

I must admit that although the shotgun approach sometimes works, I personally prefer the other, more precise method. I have always found that in the majority of cases, a carefully planned approach to specific companies is far more successful.

This approach is also far more effective when you are looking to develop strategic alliances between companies from specific sectors, as we saw in the last chapter.

Think about it. For most people, from a time point of view, it's quite difficult to conduct in-depth research into more than a couple of dozen companies at a time. Even with the aid of the Internet, securing the range of background information that will help you put together an approach that relates to a company's genuine marketing needs will take considerable time. In my opinion, the best way to go about targeting is to adopt the rifle approach and spend your time effectively. It ensures that you have the time to both research and, subsequently, follow up each contact that you make.

Incidentally, I've always found that research can be an extremely effective door opener. When we look at what, to many people, is the most daunting part of the sponsorship sales process – getting a meeting with a company – you'll appreciate how useful this ploy can be.

With so many companies out there, when devising a targeting strategy it is wise to establish an initial selection criteria. This will immediately help you hone in on companies that are going to hopefully provide a realistic "fit" for your opportunity, and eliminate the rest. A simplistic example of this might be a ladies football team, which is looking for a shirt sponsor. The team plays in a local county league. The problem facing the person responsible for finding sponsorship is knowing which companies to approach.

How should that person go about the task? For a start, it's unlikely that a national brand would find the opportunity of interest, as it wouldn't provide the essential geographical coverage. It would seem logical, therefore, that only companies that are situated within the county would be worth approaching. This would be the first criteria that could be set. **Criteria 1: must be based in the county.**

Next question. What is the most important entitlement that this ladies' team has to offer? Probably the opportunity for a sponsor to have its branding prominently shown on the team shirt, which would offer a potential sponsor the likelihood of reasonable local media coverage. It would make sense, therefore, for the team to introduce a second qualification factor which states that, of those companies situated within the county border, it is only the ones whose target market is situated in the county that would be appropriate. In other words, a company that might be based in the county but who specialises in export sales, would probably not find the local media coverage important. **Criteria 2: target market must be within the county.**

There are many more criteria that might be applied in this way to narrow down the targeting exercise. One might involve the type of business that would be most likely to show interest. For example, if brand awareness in the local media is the primary entitlement for the sponsor, it's not very likely that this will excite a company that manufactures church organs. To a shop that sells ladies toiletries, on the other hand, it may well be of interest. **Criteria 3: Brand awareness is important to the company.**

By continuing to apply this train of thought to the process of establishing which companies are worth approaching, you will find that, what initially looked a daunting job, now becomes more manageable.

Before you suggest that I am pre-judging companies, which I earlier stated you should never do, I want to point out that we're not excluding or pre-judging any company. All that we're doing is to create a starting point, based on companies that would be the most likely to fit your criteria. If you have no joy with the companies you initially target, extend the criteria slightly to include some of those that weren't selected. If you continue to do this, you'll eventually cover virtually all possibilities.

In this way, you will hopefully discover that it isn't too difficult to select a list of companies that might find your sponsorship opportunity relevant to their marketing activities. You need to narrow your targeting down to a number of companies that you can approach individually and follow up in the manner that is necessary to bring them on board. The criteria that you apply will vary from situation to situation, but it is well worth taking some time to draw up such a list. If you don't, you'll find yourself wasting a great deal of time further down the road.

This brings us to another targeting process that I have always found works extremely effectively and can be easily combined with what we have just covered. It's called "targeting by sector".

Targeting by sector

There are many benefits to be gained from identifying specific categories of business and focusing your efforts on them. The FedEx deal that I mentioned earlier came about as a direct result of my decision to target the international express transportation industry.

Within the space of four months of making an initial "cold call" to both FedEx and one of its competitors, I was in the enviable position of having potential multi-million dollar deals on the table from both companies. The outcome was that, within six months of that first call, the Benetton F1 Team appeared at the British Grand Prix at Silverstone in 1997 with FedEx branding proudly emblazoned on the sidepods of its two cars. FedEx remained a major Benetton F1 sponsor until it moved to Ferrari and subsequently on to the Williams BMW team. I found that focusing on a specific industry sector in this way has several key benefits:
• It saved a great deal of time on research
• It helped me understand the needs of companies in that sector
• It helped me learn about the competition within the industry
• It helped me know who were the key players
• It helped me learn who were the up-and-coming companies
• I found out what key events take place in that industry sector, such as exhibitions, conferences, etc.
• I better understood the problems facing the industry sector
• I was soon able to talk the language of the companies operating in that sector
• I was able to generate greater respect because of this.

Targeting by sector can be very helpful when you sit down to plan your contact strategy. It can also play a helpful role in developing multi-dimensional sales plans, which offer the advantage of effective business-to-business opportunities for participating companies.

There is no doubt that the whole business of targeting and research has become much easier today than it was for much of my career, the reason being the availability of the Internet. Instead of having to wade through trade directory after trade directory at your local library, as most of us did in those days, you can now work from the comfort of your own home in a far quicker, more effective fashion.

Collating news articles from the business pages of newspapers and magazines can provide vital leads when selecting the companies you are going to approach. Most publications today have an online version, which carries many of the headlines and major stories. If you choose the right media sources to match your targeting criteria, you can compile a highly effective list of potential sponsors.

Whether you are targeting on a local, national or international basis, the principle is the same: look for stories that could provide useful information. One area that I refer to a great deal is "people on the move" within the business sections of newspapers and magazines. If you see that your local furniture store has a new branch manager, there's a good chance that he will want to introduce some new ideas. That means he might be receptive to the idea of a creative sponsorship opportunity.

You read about a company opening their first new branch in your area. Maybe they will be looking for promotional ideas. It's worth a try and it should be possible to identify some aspects of your sponsorship opportunity that might be perfect for a company in that situation. Other sources of inspiration for compiling your target list could include:

• Marketing magazines
• Sports marketing publications
• Chamber of Commerce newsletter
• Trade associations (for targeting by sector)
• Business exhibitions
• Advertisements
• Employment advertisements (informs you of company expansion)
• Existing sports sponsors
• Sports arena advertisers
• Personal referrals from friends and families.

If you compile your target list in a systematic manner, aimed at quality rather than quantity, you will reap the benefits in due course. I usually target eight to ten companies at a time, finding that this gives me the best chance to research and follow up on an individual basis. If companies drop out, you can just replace them with another that meets your criteria and thereby keep the project manageable.

Once you have compiled a list of companies that match your criteria, you will need to find out some fundamental information about them, before making your initial sales approach. In the next chapter, I'm going to look at the sort of information that will help you gain an insight into what is important to them from a marketing perspective.

Unless you can get under the skin of a company and appreciate how they look at their marketing, you'll always battle to convince them to speak to you, let alone to set up a meeting.

SUMMARY

You have a choice of adopting a shotgun or a rifle approach to targeting potential sponsors. The problem with the shotgun approach is that, although it allows you to communicate with perhaps hundreds of companies at a time, it won't be quality contact.

By adopting a more focused approach, you will be able to conduct vital research into each company before making contact. You will also find that you can manage the tasks of following-up more efficiently if you only have ten or so contacts on the go at any one time.

Chapter 10

What do you **need** to **know?**

I find it a sobering thought that I had already left school when the sports sponsorship revolution started back in 1968, with Colin Chapman negotiating that famous Gold Leaf Team Lotus sponsorship deal. I'm often asked what I think has been the most significant change during the intervening years that has made the sponsorship acquisition process so much harder. I find it a quite difficult question, as it's not easy to identify just one area. There have been so many changes over that period of time, including the incredible amount of competition faced from every other sport and from the charity, arts, educational and conservation sectors.

I think that if I were really pushed to come up with an answer to the question, it would have to be the barriers, both human and technical, that have now been put in place by companies to discourage personal communication from external sources. What I mean by this is that I always used to find it relatively straightforward to phone a company, speak to an appropriate person and within the space of a few minutes, establish whether there were grounds for progressing my proposals. That is no longer the case and it is now one of the most difficult aspects of the job.

Forgetting sponsorship for a moment, I think that it is a very sad reflection of our society in general that more and more obstacles are being put in the way of personal communication in so many areas of our lives. I'm sure that you've all suffered the interminable process that you are subjected to when you phone many large companies. You experience an endless pre-recorded selection of menus before being forced to listen to mindless musical overtures in the vain hope that somewhere at the end of this debilitating process, you might be lucky enough to be exposed to a human being.

Have you ever tried phoning back a second time and asked to speak to the person with whom you had started to share an understanding of your problem, some 30 minutes before? You have more chance of winning the Lottery! The sad result is that you often have to start from scratch again.

In so many ways in our lives, personal communication is now being discouraged and eroded. I think that as a result, the levels of frustration we endure on an almost daily basis are increasing rapidly. From conversation with friends, family and business colleagues, it becomes apparent that there are many people who are sick and tired of the way in which these impersonal systems are being forced on us. So why do we let it happen? Why do we let companies dictate to us in this way? Perhaps that's the subject of another book, so let me put the soapbox away and get back to the sponsorship sales process!

Those of you who are currently involved in marketing sponsorship opportunities must surely agree that the task of actually speaking to a meaningful contact within a business is becoming more difficult by the day.

It is so easy for people to hide behind voice and emails that it comes as quite a surprise when someone actually takes your call. Of course, I'm not so naïve as to ignore the difficulties facing companies if they were to take every call that came in, but I feel that too many of them have taken it to extremes. In the process, they are missing out on some very innovative and powerful business opportunities that they may be totally unaware of.

It always reminds me of that much-publicised cartoon, showing King Harold in his tent, cleaning his sword, on the eve of the Battle of Hastings in 1066. A messenger walks in and advises Harold that a travelling merchant is outside. He has something to show the King that he feels could help win the battle. Harold's reply, that he is far too busy cleaning his sword to be disturbed, is relayed back to the merchant, who shrugs his shoulders and loads the machine-gun back on to his cart!

"There are far too many marketing personnel within companies who have an inflated opinion of their own importance"

I recently came across a great example of the difficulty that can exist in making contact with a company. I read in the trade press that a well-known business, which produces a high volume brand of mineral water, had appointed a new marketing director. At the time, my company represented a very high profile international sports association that was offering the exclusive soft drink pouring rights at one of its major events. This meant a potentially high level of revenue for the right business. Of course, there was a level of sponsorship involved as well, but with comprehensive TV coverage, it certainly wasn't an opportunity that could be called insignificant.

I phoned the company to ask for the email address of the new director, thinking that it would be more polite to introduce myself briefly by email and outline my reason for wishing to speak to her. Sorry, we don't give out email addresses, the switchboard operator informed me. Perhaps I could speak to her PA to explain the purpose of my call, I suggested? No, she doesn't accept phone calls. Could I email her? No, you have to send a fax. Accordingly, I dusted off my now little-used fax machine and sent through a one-page letter, requesting a conversation about the potential revenue-generating opportunity.

A week went by, with no response. I decided to follow up by phone to see if the fax had been received and read by the person in question.

I explained to the switchboard operator that I had sent in a fax, as requested. Could I now speak to the PA to check that it had arrived and been read by the director? Hold on! A long wait ensued. No, she doesn't know who you are, so she won't take your call. How can I find out if the fax has been read, I asked? I was told that I must send in another fax, asking if my previous ones had been read!

I put together another communication, politely enquiring whether the fax had been read and if there was an interest in finding out more detail. Guess what? No response. To this day, I still don't know whether my faxes were read. How long would it have taken for that PA to send out a one-line email, thanking me for the opportunity but declining the offer, or telling me that they hadn't had time to look into the matter as yet? Twenty seconds maximum!

Call me old-fashioned, but I think that the way in which this was handled simply displayed a lack of manners. It wasn't as though this was an insignificant association on whose behalf I was making the approach, and it was most certainly not an insignificant revenue generating opportunity for the company. Sadly, manners in many businesses seem to be very much in decline and I have to assume that it emanates from the top. I personally find that there are far too many marketing personnel within companies who have an inflated opinion of their own importance and feel that bad manners are acceptable. I believe that we all have a job to do, and if we treat people as we ourselves would like to be treated, it would make all of our lives easier and more pleasant.

My worst, though, is people who spend half their lives telling you how incredibly busy they always are. I'm sure you all know some of these. It's as though no one else has an idea of what it is to be busy. There are people in companies who are so busy that they can't even find 20 seconds to ask their secretary to send off a short email or letter, regretting that they will not be pursuing the opportunity that you have sent to them, but thanks anyway. They consider that it is far easier just to ignore your communications and hope that you'll "go away". I don't think that it does them any favours. These very same companies are quite happy to thrust their own advertising in our faces, to bombard us with pop-ups on the Internet and to send us junk emails and direct mail by the ton. Why then, do they take offence when people want to make contact with them and try to sell them something? If we have no time for manners or respect in business, I think we are going backwards, not progressing.

Even a "no" can be a positive

Fortunately, there are still companies who recognise that if they relied only on internally generated ideas, they could be missing out on some great opportunities. As a result, they treat people who contact them with respect. I recently had reason to make contact with one of the country's largest power generators to put forward a sponsorship opportunity that I felt was appropriate. It was eventually declined, but the company's brand development manager, with whom I had been dealing, took the trouble to email with a bullet point list of the various reasons that had led her and her colleagues to this decision. She even offered to introduce me to someone in a different geographical part of the company who she felt might have an interest in what I was offering. I immediately wrote back and thanked her for this.

What a difference to my previous example. Of course, the cynical amongst you might say that it doesn't matter how, or even if, you get told "no". You could say that what mattered was that I didn't get a "yes". I'm sorry, but I totally disagree! Not only was I able to take on board the points that this person made, which helped me with my next approach, but I now have another contact within that company. In addition, a relationship has been established which means that if another opportunity comes along, I feel confident that I can approach her again. Her attitude also enhanced my opinion of her company.

I would like to say that the difficulty in establishing communication with so many companies is a rare occurrence. Unfortunately, I can't. This policy of isolation is an increasing trend in the business world. It is something that we have to find a way of managing.

Fortunately, as I have shown, there are still many companies out there in the marketplace whose senior personnel will, if approached in a professional manner, communicate with you in a pleasant, helpful way. They are aware that you are simply doing a job, the same as they are. They may also be thinking of the King Harold story that I related earlier in this chapter, and realise that the merchant offering a machine gun might just be the next caller! In other words, perhaps your proposal is just what the company has been looking for. If I had to pinpoint the one skill that I have developed which has stood me in good stead throughout my career, I would say that it has been my ability to find a way around these barriers and initiate contact with a company at the right level. I'll be sharing my methods with you a little further on when we look at the subject of "making contact". The feedback that I get from a high number of people who have attended my training courses, and others whom I have spoken to, shows that this is an aspect of the sponsorship acquisition process that they find the most difficult.

This ability to be able to talk to relevant personnel within a company is of prime importance. Whether it is to research a company, or to make contact for the purpose of setting up a meeting, you will need to be proficient at this form of communication.

In the previous chapter, we looked at ways of selecting which companies you should approach with your sponsorship opportunity. Hopefully you should be able to do a considerable amount of the initial research necessary to determine whether or not the company meets your pre-set criteria, through the use of the Internet, company reports and trade directories. However, once you have identified a manageable number of companies that you feel potentially meet your criteria, you will

"Research helps you develop ways of approaching a company – and, if done in the right way, help you find an ally within the organisation"

still need to do some more research. This time it will be research that will provide you with the information that can help get you a meeting, or at least a phone conversation, with personnel at a senior level in those companies.

Thorough research can help you to create a powerful attention-grabbing sales approach, one that is capable of generating enough interest at the right level within a company. If you take the time to work your way through a company website, you can often unearth a great deal about the business aims and philosophy of companies and, in the process, find a possible fit with your sponsorship opportunity. A statement such as "It is the intention of the ABC company to develop our business growth by establishing offices in France and Italy", can provide an opportunity for you to approach the company with a sponsorship opportunity that could provide a high profile for its services in those countries. Similarly, you might discover in the recruitment section of the company website that it is expanding its sales force. What a good opportunity to offer a sponsorship programme that includes the creation of a sales incentive programme, based on its primary activity.

Research not only helps you develop ways of approaching a company, it can also provide you with another benefit. If you go about it in the correct way, it is quite feasible to develop a good enough relationship with someone in the company that you're researching, to be able to ask them to set up an initial meeting with the appropriate decision-maker. In other words, the research process can help you find an ally within the organisation. That ally may be someone far removed from the sponsorship decision-making process, but if they can help you with the information that you are seeking, and then facilitate a meeting, what an added bonus for you.

This is what I did in a couple of the Formula 1 deals that I put together. I found an ally within each company who would answer my questions and point me in the right direction. This meant that when I eventually made my initial sales contact with the company, using the method that I describe later, I had enough information not to waste the person's time and would subsequently gain their respect for having done my homework. Such an ally can be invaluable, but it is important to respect their confidentiality. Another thing, you must not forget to thank them and keep them informed of progress.

Brian helped the Elida Gibbs brand, DENIM, commercially exploit its sponsorship of the Williams Formula 1 Team at the South African Grand Prix. Jacques Laffite (in car) and Keke Rosberg were the Team's drivers

When you start your research process, what is it that you need to find out?

For a start, I always like to know if the company has been involved in sponsorship before. If so, how did it work out? This information can do two things for you. It can save you a great deal of pain. You might discover, for example, that they recently sponsored a sports team which became insolvent midway through the season and which was unable not only to fulfil its sponsorship obligations, but was also unable to refund any part of the fee. Armed with this information, you can avoid a mighty unpleasant surprise. You can also highlight the financial soundness of your sponsorship opportunity and turn that to your advantage (assuming, of course, that it is financially sound). One way of doing this might be to build in a stage payment plan, demonstrating in the process that your sponsor remains in control of the financial situation.

On the other hand, you might find out that the company has previously been involved in quite a successful sponsorship, which came to an end purely because of a change in the direction of their own marketing. Very often, a company will decide that after a certain period of time, a sponsorship programme has delivered as much as it can and it is time to look at new opportunities, however successful it may have been.

Either way, it's important to know as much about the situation as possible. You also need to know what the geographical marketing structure is within a company. For example, is the UK marketing department responsible for marketing activities in Europe, or is that done by a separate European office? Very often you'll find that within a large organisation, each country will have its own marketing budget and decision-making process. You need to know this, particularly if you are selling a sponsorship property that includes events in both Europe and the UK.

If you are selling an international or even a global sponsorship property, it becomes even more critical to understand just how decisions are reached and budgets allocated, within any global corporations that you target. You need to know and understand how an international company that commits to a major sponsorship in a sport such as Formula 1, finances the deal. Very often, it is through mandatory contributions from the budgets of their operations in each country where they are present.

I remember carrying out an interesting sponsorship consultancy for the Unilever Group in South Africa. It came about as a direct result of this method of financing a sponsorship. Elida Gibbs, a Unilever company, took the decision to promote sales of Denim, the men's toiletry brand, through sponsorship of the Williams F1 Team. Each Elida Gibbs operation around the world had to contribute to the sponsorship fund. That was fine for the European countries within the Group, as they could leverage (commercially exploit) the sponsorship across several European Grands Prix. This could be done quite easily, because of the geographical proximity for entertaining VIP guests and for running promotions within retail stores. For example, Denim in France would benefit from the European media coverage of the French, Italian, German, Monaco, Belgian, Spanish and even the British races and could also use these as a basis for sales promotions and possible entertaining. In this way, they might amortise their expenditure across up to half a dozen Grands Prix.

For Elida Gibbs in South Africa, it was far more difficult to justify its financial investment, as its marketing department had to make the most of their commercial mileage from just one event a year: the South African Formula 1 Grand Prix at the Kyalami Circuit.

I was retained by Elida Gibbs to help the company design and implement a strategy that would assist them in generating as much brand awareness as possible whilst the Williams F1 team was in South Africa. This involved the creation and execution of a number of innovative promotions, media events and sales incentive programmes. I also had to ensure that we made full use of the teams' two drivers at that time, Keke Rosberg and Jacque Laffite. The work that I did gave me a good insight into some of the issues facing a company when it is considering what amounts to an international sponsorship.

Hopefully, this will demonstrate to you the importance of finding out as much as you can about the geographical structure of a company and the way in which it involves its individual satellite operations to put together a budget. If you are aware of how international sponsorships are often funded, you will be better prepared to show ways in which all the contributors can derive value from their contribution.

What else might be important to find out about a targeted company? Here are some of the information categories that I try to build into my research activities:

What are the primary target markets? (Age, gender, social status etc.)

If you don't find this out, you can waste a great deal of your own time and end up looking very amateurish. For example, it's unlikely that Saga Holidays (for the over-fifties) would be interested in becoming sponsors of a skateboarding competition. On the other hand, they could be perfect as sponsors of a bowls championship. By assessing the target audience accurately, you can save yourself a lot of unnecessary effort.

When is the marketing budget prepared, submitted and approved?

This is really critical, particularly if you are seeking a fairly large sponsorship fee. If you can work to a company's budget timetable, you are far more likely to be successful.

Who are their major competitors?

Why should this be important? Well, if you can ascertain what major marketing activities their competitors are involved in, it can often prove helpful. You'll find that many companies will try to take a different approach to their competitors. This can mean that if their main rival is already involved in sponsoring the sport in which you are involved, it's better to be aware of this and try to counter it than be totally unprepared.

Does the company use a sponsorship evaluation agency?

More and more large companies now use the services of a sponsorship agency to evaluate, advise and recommend sponsorship opportunities. If you can find out if this is the case, it will be an important factor in developing your approach strategy. It may be that you want to approach the agency first of all and get them on your side.

Which are the major media sources that the companies consider important?

If you can identify which media publications or TV and radio programmes are important to a company, it will help greatly with the way in which you position your sponsorship opportunity. Time and time again, I have found the innovative use of the media within a sponsorship sales strategy, to be a very powerful tool. If you know in advance which media sources are likely to impress a potential sponsor, it can help you to create an innovative proposal of the type that I previously outlined.

Does the company have a sales force and how is it incentivised?

One of the most underrated ways in which sponsorship can be used is as a platform for measurable sale incentive programmes. It will help you a great deal to find out the size of a company's sales force, whether the company uses sales incentive programmes and what are the rewards offered. I can promise you that few of your competitors will bother to include this opportunity within a sponsorship proposal, so time spent researching this information could prove very valuable.

How is the company website promoted?

For many companies, attracting people to their websites is of prime importance. If you can find out how they achieve this at present, it will be useful when you come to design you initial approach. Sponsorship can be a very effective platform for the promotion of a company's URL.

Are any new products going to be launched in the near future?

This is vital information, but is understandably well hidden by many companies. If you can do a Sherlock Holmes' and find out what's in store, it will add tremendous value to any proposals that you make.

Are any new branches going to be opened?

It may well be that if a company is opening a new branch, it will be looking at some innovative ways of promoting it and raising awareness. Your sponsorship might just offer some interesting ways of achieving this. If you don't find this information out, you could be missing a great opportunity:
• What is the decision-making hierarchy?
• Who makes the ultimate decision?
• Who influences the decision?
• What is the decision making process?

These questions are very important. You can waste a tremendous amount of time and end up being hugely disappointed if you don't first check out this information carefully. I don't mind admitting that I've often been guilty of getting quite excited when the person that I have contacted gives out really positive signals, only to discover that this person counts for very little in the decision-making process, but likes to give out the impression that they do.

I've found that there are usually people in most companies who are more than happy to alleviate the boredom of their normal working day by talking about sport to a visitor. If you take it on their word that they are key to the decision-making process, you lay yourself open to a huge disappointment and also some major embarrassment.

If you research in advance who is important and who isn't, it will be extremely helpful to you. However, the fact that a person isn't the decision-maker doesn't mean that you should leave them out of your plans. They may well be part of the decision-influencing process. Knowing how decisions are reached and which people are part of the process, is valuable information and well worth considerable effort on your part in obtaining it.

Once you have found out who the appropriate people are, you ideally need to do some research on them. If you can find out some background on these people, such as where they worked previously, or what their sporting interests are, it can help you approach them in an effective way and also can help in planning your meetings with them.

As I mentioned earlier in the book, you will sometimes come across opportunities during your research activities to initiate your sales approach. Just be a little careful that you don't get dragged in to a decision-making process before you are ready. If you're not prepared, you can sometimes find yourself face-to-face with the right person, but because you haven't yet worked out ways in which your property can prove beneficial, you'll quickly end up with a negative response. It's fair to say that the more experienced you become, the better you'll be able to turn such situations to your advantage.

I could go on and on with this list of information, which I believe is worth researching, but there comes a time when you have to say enough is enough. You can devote too much time to researching. I recall spending some time in America, helping to train a very hard-working and earnest young sponsorship salesman. He had been employed by a sponsorship agency that represented one of the top American IndyCar teams. His role was to secure sponsors for the team.

He was a very bright lad, with a high level of determination. He certainly wasn't scared of hard work and realised that preparation and thorough research ensured a sound foundation of a good sponsorship sales strategy. I flew over to the US once a month and usually met with him to see how he was progressing. I was always very impressed by the incredible amount of research that he had carried out on a company that had been targeted. I swear that he even knew the birthdays of the president's grandchildren!

The problem was that whenever I asked him how many companies he had made appointments with, he invariably would tell me that he was still waiting to finalise the research before actually getting down to the business of setting up meetings. After six months, it became blatantly obvious that he was burying himself into the research to avoid the task of getting on the phone and trying to establish contact. His research was faultless, but was far too in-depth. At the rate he was going, by the time he eventually got to see a company, the research would be out of date. So, keep things in proportion. Research should be a vital part of your sponsorship acquisition strategy, but you must recognise that there has to be a time when you pick up that phone and start acting as a salesperson.

SUMMARY

Research is essential if you are to gain a company's interest in what you have to offer. You can avoid a number of pitfalls by researching any previous sponsorship history. If you can find an ally in the company who will help you understand the way in which the company operates and how the management is structured, it can prove invaluable. You need to be able to develop an attention-grabbing introduction to your sales approach and careful research can help provide this.

If you go about it in an innovative way, your research can help you establish a meeting with the decision-maker at the appropriate time. By developing contacts within the company from a research point of view, you can encourage them to introduce you to the decision-makers when you are ready.

What can **help you?**

A t the beginning of this book, I explained how I had put together my very first sponsorship deal, enabling me to race in Formula Ford. Following that deal, my racing career had been running quite well, without setting the world alight, for about three years. I'd been competing in Formula Ford 1600 and really needed to take a decision as to what to do the following season. At that time, I was still competing very much on an amateur basis and I was employed as the UK sales training director for the American ITT Corporation. Thanks to a chance meeting, my life was about to change direction in a big way.

Earlier that year, I had negotiated a sponsorship deal with ITT, which would allow the company to promote its in-house magazine, called ITT Focus, through my racing activities. This publication was distributed to all of its European employees. In addition, I'd agreed a small sponsorship deal with a garage in Maidstone, which would enable its staff to prepare my racing car. It was while I was at the garage one day, helping my mechanic load my Hawke DL11 onto its trailer, that a driver who had stopped for petrol, wandered over to take a look at the car.

As so often happens when people see a single-seater racing car up close, he wanted to know how fast it was, what engine it had, where did I race it and so on. He was about to return to his car when I decided to find out a bit more about him and what he did for a living. It turned out that he was employed by a company called SodaStream. Some of you may know that SodaStream was an appliance that let you make fizzy soft drinks at home.

Sensing that this could be worthwhile, I then persuaded him to park his car and come back and have a chat, also offering him the chance to sit in the Hawke. I knew that once he was in, it would be quite tricky for him to get out of the small cockpit and I would have a captive audience for a few minutes. A useful ploy! In the course of the conversation, in which he told me about SodaStream, it transpired that there had just been a management buy-out from Kenwood, who were the manufacturers of the SodaStream equipment. SodaStream was now a stand-alone company in its own right. We continued chatting, until I eventually showed him how to climb out of the car.

Four months later, I was able to conclude a sponsorship deal that was almost certainly the largest that had ever been achieved within Formula Ford. The deal was worth £25,000 at a time when the typical budget for running a professional Formula Ford team was around £12,000-£15,000. I think that I was also one of the very first competitors to arrive at the track with one of the large transporters that are so much the norm these days.

Later in this book I have included a detailed case study, outlining the way in which I was able to put this sponsorship deal together. Although the SodaStream sponsorship took place a long time ago, the way in which I structured and presented the opportunity is as valid today as it was then. It encapsulates many of the points that I have already covered as being vital ingredients, if your proposals are to be taken seriously by a company.

"Keep very quiet about contacts you have or are working on. Don't talk to anyone about a possible deal until it is signed, sealed and paid for"

The deal that I concluded with SodaStream meant that I would have to seriously consider whether I could now combine my full-time job with a national racing programme which would take me all over the country. I decided that it was a once-in-a-lifetime opportunity. If it didn't work out, I could always find another job, and so I made the decision to leave ITT and concentrate on a full-time career in motor racing. To help bring in some further income, I became an instructor at the new racing driver school that had just been started at the Thruxton racetrack in Hampshire.

Sadly for me, the car that I chose to compete in that year could best be described as an absolute dog! It's little consolation to me now, but that car effectively proved to be the death knell for its manufacturer. The previous season, the Hawke DL15 had been the car to drive, winning just about everything in the hands of two drivers who were to go on to Grand Prix careers, Derek Warwick and Derek Daly. It seemed the logical conclusion to opt for its radical successor, the DL17. It proved to be a disaster, as all of the drivers who competed in it will confirm. One of these fellow sufferers was an infamous celebrity in his own right. It was none other than Roy James, who had been convicted as one of the great train robbers. He was better known as "the weasel".

Prior to serving 12 years of what I think was a 30-year prison sentence for his part as the getaway driver in the robbery, Roy had been a successful racing driver, competing in Formula Junior. He was a silversmith by trade and, while inside, designed and produced several silver trophies, which he later presented to various motor racing clubs.

When he had served his sentence, he decided to try to get back into racing and tested a Formula Atlantic car at Silverstone. The rumour going around the pits at the time was that he was sponsored by British Rail! Such is the black humour in motorsport.

Unfortunately for him, Roy ended up crashing the car and breaking his arm, so he stepped down a category and bought a Hawke DL17 Formula Ford, competing in the same national championship as me. Throughout that season, I found him a very tough and competitive racer, but perhaps not surprisingly, an extremely quiet, intense individual. The only time I ever saw Roy become emotional was when he joined several of us in complaining bitterly to the manufacturer about this unbelievably poor racing car, that we had each bought. I think the experience that year put him off racing and I don't recall him ever getting into a race car again.

The final word on my SodaStream sponsorship is not included in the case study. It concerns a lesson that I learned the hard way. Those of you who have been involved in the sponsorship business for some time may well be able to endorse what I am about to relay from your own experiences. If you are fairly new to sponsorship-seeking, take note and you may avoid what happened to me.

Towards the end of that SodaStream season, I had a long chat with Don Philpot, the man who I had met at the garage. I had a lot of time for Don, who was an amazing character, full of energy and enthusiasm. I asked his opinion of what I should do. It was obvious that the racing hadn't gone as well as planned. We seriously considered changing manufacturer mid-way through the season, but the promises that were being made to us about improvements that were supposedly in the pipeline, stopped us from doing this until it was too late. His feedback from the board was that they were very happy with the results of the sponsorship, particularly in respect of a measurable increase in sales activity, attributable to store promotions that we had carried out. He informed me that everyone understood the car problems that year and we started to talk about the possibility of moving up to Formula 3 the following season. It looked promising, but then I was young and quite naïve. It hadn't dawned on me that other people would try to take the sponsorship away from me.

This is exactly what happened when John Webb, then the boss of Brands Hatch, approached SodaStream and persuaded them to stop sponsoring an individual and instead become the title sponsor of the proposed Sports 2000 Championship that was to be launched the following season.

While I think it was actually quite a good move from SodaStream's point of view, it was the way in which it was done that hurt. I had worked hard to introduce SodaStream into motorsport and I felt that John Webb could have somehow included me in the deal. How green was I? Unfortunately, Don Philpot, who had been such a staunch supporter and good friend, died unexpectedly that year and I lost out in the overall scheme of things. It was a lesson that I have never forgotten.

My later years in Formula 1 also hardened me to the way in which people in big-time sport operate. Where there is a lot of money, there will always be people prepared to do anything to get their hands on it. My advice to anyone involved in looking for sponsorship is to keep very quiet about whatever leads or contacts you have or are working on. Whatever you do, don't talk to anyone about a possible deal until it is signed, sealed and paid for. You'd be amazed how many people are out there looking for funds for some activity or other. It may not be for the sport that you are in, in fact it may not even be for sport, but if they hear you mention that a certain company is considering spending some money, they will be in like a shot. Believe me, I do the same!

I stressed earlier the importance of thorough research. It's worth mentioning that one of the factors that helped me present such a strong sponsorship case to SodaStream was the research that I did on that company, particularly on its specific marketing needs as a new management buy-out operation.

The opportunity to research is so much easier today than it was before the launch of the Internet. It really is quite an incredible research tool. If you are prepared to use some initiative, you can find out the most amazing amount of information about a company. What I have found, though, is that many of the well-known companies are very cagey about putting people's name and contact details on their site. If this is the case, you might get more joy by working through a Chamber of Commerce membership list or a trade association, whose sites can be very useful. I must admit that there are few companies that I've come across who cover their tracks very thoroughly, however hard they might try not to divulge contact information. You just need to use some initiative and try different routes.

If you're researching companies that are close to you geographically, it's well worth trying to make friends with someone in the local media. They tend to be a fount of local knowledge and if you can get the business reporters of the paper, radio and even TV station on your side, they can be very helpful.

Another obvious, but effective, source of research information is a company's annual report. You'll find that some larger public libraries keep these in their reference section. They can be very effective in extracting information about directors and in gaining an insight into a company's future plans.

However much you are able to find out on the Internet and in other ways, there will often still be a need to make direct contact with a company, to find out certain information. This can be tricky, as you will invariably be asked why you want the information. In these situations, you have to be a little creative. A method that I find works well is to get one of the secretaries on your side. If you go about this in a professional way, they can be a great source of information about what goes on in a company, but there is a very fine line between patronising them and encouraging them to provide you with some very useful information. So, which secretaries should you contact and how do you get them to provide you with information?

In terms of initial research, as opposed to making my sales approach, the most successful route for me has been to phone a company and specifically ask for the secretary to the sales manager. It's my experience that sales department personnel, if approached carefully, will have more sympathy for what you are trying to do. This is probably because they face the same problem themselves and are more inclined to help you. Sales secretaries, in my experience, tend to be fairly open-minded people. They have to be as they are probably dealing with some fairly outgoing individuals.

> *"There are few companies who cover their tracks very thoroughly, however hard they might try not to divulge contact information"*

If you can develop a contact in this way within a company, you can usually find out a lot of the information that you want in terms of target markets, sales incentives, promotions and geographical structures. If you are really persuasive, you can encourage the secretary to eventually use her contacts within the company to arrange a meeting for you with the decision maker or key influencer. What a pleasure! You avoid that difficult job of approaching them from cold.

There is often a network of secretaries within a company and if you can break into that and make a good impression with one of them, they can make your route through the company so much easier. The real key is the way that you deal with them. If you're over familiar, you have no chance. If you treat them as a junior or an obstacle in your way, you have no chance. Treat them with respect and be aware of what an important role they play and you can make a very good contact for yourself.

You are going to get tired of this, but I am not going to apologise for reminding you to thank them. I find that people can be very helpful and if you take the trouble to thank them – and also to let them know what progress you are making as a result of their assistance. They will very much appreciate that. I've asked a number of secretaries if they mind being asked for help in the way that I've outlined. Their reply, almost without exception, has been that they are only too glad to be treated as an intelligent human being, not some mindless barrier that tries to stop people talking to their boss. Many of them then went on to say that their only criticism is that, too often, they never receive any thanks from the person that they have tried to help.

SUMMARY

The sponsorship business can be extremely competitive and it pays to keep all of your negotiations strictly confidential until you have a signed agreement in place.

The SodaStream deal that I negotiated came about due to many factors, one of which was the thorough research that was carried out, which enabled me to make an attention-grabbing approach.

It pays to develop contacts while you are researching. These can prove very helpful when you are ready to make your sales approach. The secretaries in a company are a valuable source of assistance if you go about it the right way and treat them as individuals, with a knowledge of what goes on in the company, rather than as a barrier to be overcome.

Creative **selling tools**

So far in the development of a sponsorship sales strategy we have covered four important steps:
1. The creation of a sponsorship property that is saleable and priced in a market-related way.
2. The creation of a multi-dimensional sales plan capable of generating interest within companies.
3. The targeting of companies through the use of specific criteria.
4. The research into those companies that have been selected, to determine key information.

The next step in the your sponsorship marketing strategy should be to decide what sales tools you are going to need. By sales tools, I am referring to anything that adds weight to your approach to a potential sponsor.

Sales tools can vary enormously. Looking back on my first sponsorship, the Victoria's Night Club deal, I suppose you could say that my racing car was an effective sales tool, because I used it to help me grab the decision-maker's attention. Typical sales tools might include:
• A visual presentation for use on a laptop
• Testimonials from previous sponsors
• A CD-Rom introducing the sponsorship opportunity
• A hard copy of the laptop presentation
• A colour brochure
• An artist's impression of what the branding will look like on your racing car or sponsorship property
• A press cuttings portfolio
• Case studies of successful sponsorships
• TV viewing statistics
• Audience demographics
• Event video footage.

When I define a sales tool as anything that adds weight to your approach to a potential sponsor, I am not just referring to something that you take with you to your first meeting, such as a brochure or a laptop presentation. You can also use sales tools innovatively to secure such a meeting in the first place. For example, many sponsorship seekers send out a brochure as part of their initial approach. In my book, that's a sales tool.

Over the years, I've seen some very innovative and highly effective sales tools that were used to attract attention, generate interest and secure an initial meeting. Some of these have been very simple, others far more elaborate. One in particular that I remember receiving while working for Bath Rugby Union Club, was simply a packet of grass seed. It was stylishly presented in a silver foil packet, with a clear, see-through front. On it was a label that had been personalised to show a Bath player and the club's logo. The packet had been sent by a company that wanted to help Bath commercially develop its brand. It came with a compliment slip, on which there was a message. As I recall, the wording went something like this:

• We'd like to pitch for your business
• We'd like to help you grow your business
• In the meantime, we hope that this will help you grow your pitch.

Not the most complex sales tool, but it raised a smile within the club and achieved its aim. A meeting was arranged, probably more out of curiosity as to who could have composed such a naff poem than what the company could offer. It didn't matter what the reason was. The objective was achieved.

Some months ago, I received a package in the post. On opening it, I found a bar of Kit Kat and a typed letter on high-quality company headed paper. The letter started something like this:

"Dear Brian Sims,
As a busy executive, I am sure that you have little time to read through all of your mail every day. I thought that you might like to 'take a break' and enjoy this Kit Kat with a cup of coffee while I outline briefly to you the services that my company offers."

The letter then went on to explain that this company was involved in creating stylish, eye-catching corporate identities for small to medium-sized businesses.

I liked the approach. I thought that it showed some humour and was different. It certainly caught my eye. There was only one problem. It didn't look like the version that I've shown you; in the original, my name was spelt wrong, the address was incorrect and there were no less than three spelling mistakes in the first two paragraphs. What was the name of this company? First Impressions! A great idea, undone by sloppy attention to detail. Would I want my corporate identity handled by this company? I would take some convincing.

Time and time again, I am sent letters (and emails) introducing a business service or product, often accompanying a sales tool, such as a brochure or proposal. I find that a large percentage of these have my name spelt wrong, usually with two "m"s or more often Brain instead of Brian. It's not unusual to find that there are also spelling and grammatical mistakes in the main body of the communication. You might argue that it shouldn't matter, as long as it can be understood. Wrong! It matters very much in this business. There is a good chance that the decision-maker in a company will see it, even if it's sent initially to a secretary. It could well be that he or she believes that bad spelling in a communication shows a lack of respect. Why take that chance? It's not worth it. Get it right.

A problem with emails is that many people don't bother to consider the impression that their communication sends out to the recipient. You might be in a rush to send the email off and so you dispense with pleasantries, such as "Hello" or "Hi", "Thank you" or "Kind regards". Too often the language in emails is curt and can easily be misinterpreted by the recipient as being rude or offhand. If you are going to use an email in a sales situation, take extra care to ensure that it can't be misinterpreted in any way and that the spelling, grammar and punctuation are all correct. In fact, whenever you make contact with the outside world, whether by letter, email, or even a note on a compliment slip, pay attention to detail. With spell-check facilities on computers, it shouldn't be that difficult to avoid some of the howlers that I regularly receive.

Getting back to sales tools, at the other end of the spectrum from those that I have just described, I've seen some that have cost a lot of money and failed to deliver their objective. These include videos that have been produced at great expense and which were far too long. They only succeeded in boring the intended audience. I've seen brochures that must have cost a small fortune, simply thrown in the waste bin by marketing personnel. Don't fall into the trap of thinking that if it's expensive, then it must be good. The problem with expensive sales tools is that you feel obliged to use them, even though the situation might not warrant their use.

I've explained that some sales tools can be very effective in securing a meeting for you. I've given you a couple of examples of these. While I am all for innovation, my advice is that you need to have a talent for creativity if you are going to adopt this type of approach. If you are not careful, it can easily backfire on you and look very tacky or even amateurish. That doesn't mean that you can't be a bit zany if you have the skill to do it, but it might be better to solicit the help of someone who is perhaps better qualified than you in this respect.

Sales tools are there to bring in to play only if you need them to support what you are saying. They should not be a crutch. I have always found that the most effective sales tools that I have with me are my two ears. By asking questions and then listening to the answers, you will learn so much that will help you fit your product to a prospect's real needs. If you also use your eyes and watch a person's body language, you will know if you are getting through to them. If you can see that you aren't, try a different route. Don't just plough on regardless.

Having stressed the importance of using sales tools sparingly and only at the appropriate time, there is no doubt that they do have an important role to play. What I want to do next is to look at how some of them can be designed, and used, to deliver the maximum impact.

Brochure

A great deal of money can be spent in the design and production of a full colour brochure. Dependent upon your budget and also the number of times that it is going to be used, this can be a very powerful marketing or sales tool. I would recommend such an investment, for example, in the case of a sports venue promoter, who needs to sell everything from event sponsorship to corporate hospitality, and from arena to programme advertising. There will be a need for quite a high number of these, so the cost can be effectively amortised.

As with Formula 1, there could be a level of expectation for a quality brochure if you are operating at the very top end of the market. It would look rather unimpressive to distribute a brochure that looks as though it was designed and printed at home. On the other hand, I wouldn't suggest that a young karter, who is seeking sponsorship to move into a junior formula of motor racing, necessarily needs to spend a lot of money in this way.

One major problem is that an expensive brochure cannot be personalised easily in the same way that a PowerPoint presentation can. With good quality colour printers now so inexpensive, there is no reason why you can't put together a professional-looking presentation, personalised to the company to whom you are presenting. You can even bind it yourself, with machines costing as little as £30.

I want to add, however, that there are no hard and fast rules on this. What might work for one person, doesn't always work for another. I'm not saying that you shouldn't use a nicely designed brochure. I just think that unless you have money to spare, you can use it far more effectively.

If you do decide that a brochure is appropriate, there are some guidelines that help in making it powerful and dynamic. Unless you are trained in graphic design, you will need to use a professional designer. Make sure that you brief the person well, so that what is designed is sales orientated. Insist that it contains a range of potential marketing opportunities, rather than simply filling the brochure with lots of lovely colour pictures of competitive sports or yourself. You need to demonstrate in a graphic manner that the opportunity can be used to promote many potential aspects of a company's marketing mix. These can include all of the points that we saw in the chapter on creating a saleable property, such as brand awareness, image transfer, case study development and PR.

In this way, you will be far more likely to sow a seed in the mind of anyone looking at the brochure, as opposed to simply providing a collection of colourful action pictures that will do little to generate a meaningful level of interest.

A sales presentation

I know that there are going to be many of you who will disagree with my thoughts on what constitutes a powerful, effective sales presentation. You will argue that, with modern technology, there are many really dynamic ways of producing an all-singing, all-dancing presentation, that has sound, special effects, action and colour. You'll tell me that good old Microsoft PowerPoint has had its day. And you're right. There are many ways of producing a really high-class audio-visual presentation. There are some circumstances where this is what's needed. If you are going to invite a number of companies to a presentation, as an example, prior to following them up individually, or if you are well into discussions with a company and you have been asked to present to the board, it may well be worth looking at a such a personalised, dynamic presentation to really bring the atmosphere of your sport into the formality and tranquillity of the boardroom.

Perhaps you want to distribute a CD-Rom in conjunction with a brochure that you have

"A sales presentation should be designed only to provide support for you in presenting your proposals, not to replace your own input"

produced. I know that such a method can be very effective. I've also seen some that are far too long and don't allow the prospect to jump backwards and forwards within the presentation to discuss key points. When I talk about these high-powered audio-visual programmes, I'm going to include the production of a video or DVD presentation within this category.

However, before the majority of you think that, unless you spend a lot of money on a presentation, you'll have no chance of competing with those who have the budget to make this happen, don't despair! Even some of the most expensive presentations that I've seen have failed to achieve what they set out to do. On the other hand, I have personally been able to secure some high-value sponsorship agreements using what I consider to be powerful presentations, which I've designed and produced myself, with nothing more than a scanner, a PC with PowerPoint and a little creativity.

Coming back to the point that I made earlier, a sales presentation, however costly, is still only a sales tool. It should be designed only to provide support for you in presenting your proposals, not to replace your own input. It's highly unlikely that it will sell your sponsorship proposal on its own. Only you can do that. If you remember that, you'll put the role of the presentation into perspective.

However, if you are going to the expense and effort of producing a really multi-dimensional audio-visual presentation, or perhaps a specially produced video, there are a couple of important aspects that I want to highlight, which will hopefully save you from making some of the mistakes that I did on the occasions when I took this route.

I want you to imagine that you have put together what you consider to be a really interesting, dramatic, colourful, even noisy, video presentation. It lasts for ten minutes. You show it to your colleagues, friends and family for their comments. They all like it.

The following day you are in the boardroom of a potential sponsor. You have your laptop on the table and the three directors are sat around it. The video starts and you watch their reaction. Unfortunately, what seemed like a very exciting, punchy, short, to the point, production when you sat in your own lounge to watch it, cheered on by family and friends, now seems to go on for ever and ever. The noise levels suddenly seem inappropriate. The signals coming from the audience are not good. They start looking at their watches and you begin to feel uncomfortable. With three more minutes to go in the presentation, it feels as though you have been watching it for half an hour already. Do you persevere or do you switch it off? You're in a quandary. I know that this is true because I've made this same mistake. You'll find that the majority of senior business people do not have the time or the inclination to sit through several minutes of what I always call a "scene-setting" video. When you are sitting in a business environment, watching for even three minutes can seem a long time. What adds to the problem is that it is very unlikely that the video will be personalised specifically to that company. It will almost certainly be general in what it covers.

That is one of the reasons why I think you need to be careful about the format you use. I like to remain in control of any presentation that I'm making. With a video, or similar presentation, it isn't always easy to do that. With a PowerPoint presentation, you can quickly move forward to a point that is of interest, if you feel that you are losing impact. Alternatively, you can go back to re-emphasise a specific point that you want to make. Using a modular approach to its design, it is easy to maintain this essential level of control. If you sense that the audience is familiar with certain information that you are presenting to them, confirm this with them and move on to the next module.

There is another point that is worth thinking about with an expensive audio-visual presentation. They can date very quickly. Once you have produced your masterpiece, it is usually quite tricky, expensive and time consuming to edit it. Suppose, for example, a couple of weeks after its completion, you manage to secure a sponsorship deal from a high profile media source, such as a daily newspaper. This can play an important role in any presentation that you are making to companies, but if your video is now complete, all you can do is to talk about the new deal after the presentation, perhaps losing some of the impact that it would have made if included in your show. With a simpler presentation, you can drop in a couple of new slides, as you require them.

To summarise on audio-visual presentations, my advice is to keep them very short. Use action footage from your sport purely as 10-15 second intervals between outlining ways in which the sponsorship is able to provide a range of marketing opportunities. In this way, the audience won't get bored and the action can provide powerful message support. Remember that it is not going to sell your sponsorship for you, so be very clear as to what its purpose is and why you are using it.

Now to the more often used PowerPoint style of presentation. Although PowerPoint is a fairly basic and simple format to use, that doesn't mean that it has to be dull. Far from it. With some of the money that you save by not going for a costly, audio-visual presentation, it is worth investing in some professional-standard photographs from either a good agency or an individual who you know, so that you can graphically get your message across. Perhaps you will have some of your own, but be careful about copyright infringement. You never know who might see the presentation.

Start off the design of your presentation by getting a large sheet of paper and create a flow chart of the various primary modules (or chapters) that you want to include. Such a presentation for the marketing department of a rugby club might include these major headings:
• Introduction
• The proposal
• Presentation contents
• The team: background/history
• The team: future programme

- The sponsorship opportunity
- Sponsorship entitlements
- Potential benefits
- Media statistics
- Summary.

Secondly, within each of these headings, put down in bullet point format the main points that you want to put across.

Only when you have done this should you start putting these thoughts onto the computer. In this way, you'll have a good framework in which to build up the presentation into a colourful, interesting yet clear communication of your sponsorship opportunity. It's easier to produce the text initially and then the photographs, rather than the other way round.

"The presentation will not sell the sponsorship by itself. It should provide enough information so that your prospect will want to know more"

I first started working with PowerPoint in 1996. I had just been appointed as head of motorsport sponsorship for Alan Pascoe's API Agency. I had to learn quickly how to put a computerised presentation of this sort together, because it was my job to secure sponsorship in a short space of time for the agency's new client, the Benetton Formula 1 Team. I must give credit to a very good friend of mine, Matthew Argenti, another of the Formula Ford racers that I regularly competed against back in my early career, who was managing director of the API agency at that time. He looked at my early attempts to produce a dynamic sales presentation, using PowerPoint and while he liked the graphic style that I had developed, he would tell me that there were about twice as many words in it as there should be. Time and time again, I would whittle it down until eventually I had a document that he felt was really concise, yet graphically powerful. It is a lesson that has stood me in good stead ever since and I must thank him for that.

I am shown many sales presentations and I find that a high number are too wordy by far. All that a presentation should do is to support what you are offering, not tell the whole story, word by word. You need to provide those words, as and when appropriate, within your sales meeting. The presentation should simply be there to help you move through your proposal.

I would never recommend that you send your presentation, in hard copy format, to a prospective sponsor on its own, without you being there to add voice. However, if circumstances dictate that you need to, the same still applies. Don't make it too wordy. It's always been my experience that the majority of business people, certainly at the level that you are approaching, will not bother to read through long-winded documents. They will simply put them to one side and almost invariably never get round to looking at them again. They prefer punchy, short, sharp and clearly laid out reasons as to why they would want to find out more details of the opportunity being presented.

I keep coming back to an important point. The presentation will not sell the sponsorship by itself. Its primary objective should be to provide enough information so that your prospect will want to know more. No less and no more than that.

There is a final point I would like to make before we look at some of the other sales tools. If you are going to show the PowerPoint presentation on your laptop, or with the use of a projector, make sure that you don't overdo the use of special effects. By this, I mean that if you want to "fly in" words or lines of text, don't overdo it. By doing so, you will lose the impact that can be achieved if the animation is used sparingly. A whole presentation in which the audience is faced with every line flying in, can be very tedious, and in extremes can make people feel nauseous.

I nearly forgot! If you are going to use a laptop presentation, always make sure that you have a back-up copy on CD with you, so that in the event of a disaster with your own laptop, you can use a PC within the client's own facility. Common sense, but it can easily throw you completely if you haven't prepared for this eventuality.

Other sales tools

The AA or RAC employee who has come out to fix your puncture at the side of road will certainly come prepared for most eventualities. The same should apply to you when you go to your first meeting with a company.

It shouldn't be too difficult to plan in advance what questions might come up in the meeting. For example, there is a good chance that a potential sponsor will want to know the profile of the people who will be watching the sporting event in which you are competing. By this, I mean age groups, social rating, gender and so on. It is probable that questions will be asked about the media coverage of the event. If you have to keep replying to these questions with a comment that you don't have that information with you, but that you can send it on, you will lose a great opportunity. By the time that information arrives on his desk, he may well have lost the initial enthusiasm that you had generated at that meeting. You may not get the chance of another meeting, so don't take the risk. It's better to take along supporting documents with you, even if you never have to use them.

Similarly, you should always be in a position to support statements that you make in your presentation. Again, if you can't do this while he is seemingly interested and listening to what you have to say, you may well have lost a great opportunity to progress matters. This might well apply to testimonials. If you have some worthwhile letters or documents from a previous contented sponsor, or media sources that you may have worked with within a sponsorship programme, use them. You might include some "one-liners" from these in your sales presentation, but it will be impressive if you have the full letters in a separate folder which you can leave if appropriate.

The same goes for media coverage. If you have generated an impressive amount of media coverage, a well-presented PR folder can prove very effective. A word of advice on this, however. Remember that you are presenting to a businessperson, not necessarily a sports enthusiast. While they might enjoy sport personally, in their business capacity it may well be the case that they are far more impressed by media coverage in the lifestyle section of a county magazine than on the sports pages of your local newspaper. Similarly, generating coverage in the business section of a paper can be quite powerful for the right prospect. Very often, an article about sports on the sports pages will get lost. An article which relates to sport, but which approaches the subject from a different angle and which is in the main body of the paper, as opposed to the sports pages, can often be more impressive to a potential sponsor.

As an example, an article about the way that a racing driver trains to cope with excessive g-forces, has the capability of getting into the lifestyle section of a local paper. You saw earlier how I generated a feature in the South African press on how a competitor goes about finding sponsorship. That got into a Sunday newspaper supplement.

It may be that you are seeking sponsorship for an event. If you can show a range of general interest media articles about that event in previous years, it will add weight to your proposals. It will help the prospect see what can be created and also demonstrate that you understand the importance of strong, innovative media coverage.

What other sales tools should you consider taking with you?

If you are proposing a sponsorship which includes branding, such as on a car or trackside banners, why not prepare either an artist's impression, or a computer simulation, of what that company's branding will look like in place. Anything that adds visual impact can only help.

If you are offering the sponsor a significant branding opportunity in sailing, a reasonable-sized model of the yacht, decorated in the company livery, can prove very powerful. If it helps your target individual envisage the impact that it might make, it's worth the effort and expense.

Another sales tool that I've used quite successfully has been to hand the prospect an invitation to an indoor-karting evening at a local track, enabling him to also invite a couple of colleagues. I think that this cost me £100, but was well worth it to get the prospect and some business colleagues to spend an evening with me, so that we could talk and develop a better working relationship.

If you are going to do something like this, however, make sure you get the maximum impact out of it. Don't simply throw an invitation into a conversation. My research had indicated that the person involved was quite into motor sport, so before my first meeting, I bought a model kart in a display box and attached the invitation to it. Only when I knew that the meeting was heading in a positive direction did I bring the model kart into play. I know that as soon as I had left the meeting, he was showing it to his colleagues. Had he not taken up the invitation, it would have only cost me a few pounds, but he liked the idea and we eventually went on to sign a deal. This same concept can be used in any sport and shows once again, the importance of research.

With a little imagination and creativity, there is no end to the sales tools that you can create. As long as they have a specific objective and you know how to use them effectively, I am a great believer in them. Just make sure, however, that before going into the realms of creativity, you fully prepare the range of more obvious items that you are likely to need. The TV reports, market research statistics and sponsorship evaluation surveys might not be so colourful, but they can play a vital role in your sales meeting.

One final word on the subject. When you hand an item to a prospect, whether it be a model kart or a press cuttings folder, imagine that it is very valuable. Don't just slide it haphazardly across their desk. If you give the impression that whatever you are passing across is not particularly important, that will quickly be transmitted to the prospect. You can make a cheap pen seem more valuable by the way you hand it to someone. Throw an expensive pen towards them and it will lose its value in their eyes. A small point to remember, but an important one.

SUMMARY

Sales tools can best be described as any item that you can use to enhance or support your sales activities. They can be used effectively to help you secure a meeting with a potential sponsor and also to help enhance or support your presentation at the meeting.

Sales tools should not be used as a crutch to take the place of a two-way dialogue with the prospect. Don't equate the likely effectiveness of sales tools on the cost of their production. An innovative sales tool that costs only a few pounds can often achieve more than a high-cost audio-visual presentation.

If you are working on a small budget, don't waste money on producing sales tools that can't be easily updated. Personalised presentation material is usually far more effective than that of a general nature. If you are using a video or automated slide presentation, keep it short and to the point.

If you're creating a PowerPoint presentation, make sure that it isn't too wordy. Senior business people do not have the time or inclination to read through lengthy documents. Make sure that you take with you documents that support any claims that you are making in your presentation. This can include media coverage statistics, testimonials, press cuttings and case studies of other successful sponsorships.

Chapter 5

The use of selling tools

In 1980, I decided to spend some time in South Africa. My parents had emigrated there over ten years earlier and I'd visited the country a couple of times, liking it very much. On one such occasion, in 1975, I travelled down to watch the South African Formula 1 Grand Prix at Kyalami, situated midway between Johannesburg and Pretoria.

On the flight down, I was reading Autosport when the man in the seat next to me asked me what my interest was in motorsport. I explained that I was racing Formula Fords in England and he introduced himself as Max Mosley, who is now the president of the FIA, the governing body of motorsport worldwide. In those days, he was a director of the March Formula 1 team and was on his way to the South African Grand Prix. We struck up a conversation and on more than one occasion in my subsequent career, Max has been extremely supportive and helpful to me.

It was Max Mosley who helped me land a plum job some years later, when I decided to live in South Africa for a while. Shortly after arriving in the country in 1980, I found that the Kyalami Grand Prix circuit was about to be sold. I phoned Max in the UK and asked him if he knew who the new owner was. I explained that I'd like to possibly set up a racing driver school there. Max told me to leave it with him. A few hours later, I received a phone call from Bobby Hartslief, the South African who was about to become the new owner of Kyalami. It transpired later that he had been contacted by Max Mosley, suggesting that he should meet me.

Twenty hours later, I was appointed the manager of the Kyalami Grand Prix Circuit, having only been in the country three months. It all happened so quickly that I didn't know whether to be nervous or excited. It turned out to be a great experience for me and the best thing of all was that it still allowed me time to fit in my race driving.

I learned so much in my three years at Kyalami. Working with an experienced sales team to secure sponsorship for the South African Grand Prix each year was a steep, but fascinating, learning curve. One year we had a drivers' strike, which involved many of the top F1 stars. The drivers used to stay in the same place in those days – the famous Kyalami Ranch Hotel, situated some 800 meters from the track. Formula 1 was a world apart from what it has become today. For a start, there was far more friendliness and socialising between the teams, and the public could get close to the drivers and crew members, without being treated like low-life by the security staff. During the strike, which was over an issue to do with licences, Alain Prost, Gilles Villeneuve, Ricardo Patrese, Nelson Piquet and most of the other drivers, all sat on mattresses in the bottom of the control tower while the situation was resolved. It was a hard, but useful, lesson for me to learn; explaining to the managing director of the Grand Prix's title sponsor that there might not be a race!

In 1981, I was given the chance to drive in the Kyalami 9 Hours International, a famous sports car race that attracted many of the world's top drivers, including that year, Hans Stuck, Jackie Ickx and Bob Wollek. The only problem was that I needed to bring some sponsorship with me, which is fairly normal in motor racing. In my quest, I found one company to be quite receptive, Churchill Personnel; a large recruitment agency, which had branches across the country. I met with their CEO and he put an unusual proposition to me.

"For a sponsorship to work well, the company's own staff need to buy into it. It makes such a difference in terms of renewing and extending the deal"

He told me that the previous month, the company had informed all of their staff that they wouldn't be receiving their annual pay rise that year. Business was tough and they couldn't afford to do it. He could see the many benefits of the programme that I was proposing, which incorporated a high level of guaranteed media coverage for the sponsor, as well as a competition, designed to attract high-quality, potential job seekers. However, he was worried about staff reaction, so he told me that if I wanted to secure the fee that I had proposed, I needed to attend their national sales conference, which was being staged that very weekend. Nearly all of the branch managers, all of whom were women, would be there. He was prepared to give me 30 minutes to present to these managers and to try to persuade them to support the idea of the sponsorship that I was proposing. If I got the thumbs up from them, he promised me that he would write a cheque there and then. Some challenge! I can still remember the frosty silence when I was introduced.

Fortunately, I must have got something right because I did the deal and the CEO was as good as his word. As a result, I was able to compete in one of the most exciting races that I can recall, albeit that I ended up in hospital an hour from the end of the race, when a rear wheel parted company with my car in the middle of the fourth gear, 130 mph Sunset Bend, in the pitch dark.

The Churchill Personnel deal endorsed my belief that, for a sponsorship to work well, the company's own staff need to buy into it. Once you've got them on your side, it makes such a difference to the relationship between you and the decision-maker in terms of renewing and extending the deal.

What was it that turned those women around and got them on my side? It was very simple. I didn't try to be clever and baffle them with a whole lot of marketing "speak".

I first of all explained to them that each branch would be given a supply of tickets for the race, enabling them to bring their friends and families along. This was something that I had negotiated in advance through my contacts at Kyalami. If the sponsorship deal went ahead, it would cost me about 15 per cent of the fee to purchase these tickets, even at a special price. I reckoned that 85 per cent of the fee was better than 100 per cent of nothing! I then outlined a competition that I had negotiated with The Sunday Times newspaper in South Africa, at that time the country's top-selling paper. The competition was designed to generate, for each of the Churchill regions, a database of people who were in the market for a change of job.

Suddenly, I was not quite the ogre that they had expected. They were going to see an immediate, if small, benefit for their friends and family and secondly, they could see the opportunities that the

FedEx was delivered to Benetton F1 after long, tough negotiations

database might give them to increase their branch turnover. As they could earn bonuses linked to this, it was of immediate interest. A few other benefits were presented and the outcome was that they didn't feel left out of a decision-making process. The CEO had told them that the choice was theirs. I sweated in a side room for a few minutes while the verdict was reached. Eventually the CEO walked in, with a grim look on his face. He told me that he had received the reaction of his managers and it wasn't good news. He kept a straight face and then added that it wasn't good news because he was going to have to write me a cheque!

Of course, every sponsorship negotiation is different. That is why it is so important to have as many sales tools available as you can, to cover every eventuality that might arise in your first meeting. In the last chapter, we saw that sales tools can come in all shapes and sizes. However, I don't want you to go into a meeting armed to the teeth with brochures, presentations, videos and data reports, thinking that you have to make sure that you use them all before you leave. You need to use the minimum that you require to achieve the objective of the meeting. That objective will be covered later, in the chapter on your first meeting. The sales tools are there only as backup to your dialogue with the person, or persons, that you are meeting.

Too many salespeople use sales tools as a crutch, believing that if they go through them all in order, they will have delivered a powerful argument for acceptance of their proposal. That just isn't true! I recall my very first meeting with FedEx, en route to that multi-million pound sponsorship deal for the Benetton F1 Team. I had arranged the meeting for 2.30pm at their head office in Brussels and travelled over on the Eurostar from London. I was due to meet their marketing director, Paul Evans, and their sales director. At about 2.20pm, Paul's secretary Diane, who had proved extremely helpful in securing the meeting for me, came down and told me that she was very sorry, but both men had been called into an unexpected but urgent meeting and wouldn't be available to see me. She added that if I was prepared to wait until 5.30pm, there was a chance that they might be able to see me for about 30 minutes. Not a very auspicious start to my approach for sponsorship.

The FedEx European office is situated outside Brussels, on a large business park not far from the airport, so there was nowhere to go and pass three hours. After about four coffees and a lot of newspapers, 5.30pm eventually arrived and I was shown into the marketing director's office, where

I met the two men. I had prepared what I felt was an impressive laptop presentation for them and after some initial conversation, it was agreed that I would show this to them. I don't know quite what it was that alerted me to it, perhaps experience, perhaps instinct, but I realised that this presentation wasn't having the effect that I had hoped it would. I quickly pushed it to one side and asked a straightforward question: "That's not hitting the spot, is it?" They both nodded in agreement and one of them went on to explain that they had been approached by just about every F1 team, so they knew all about the subject. He explained that no one had yet convinced them of its merits as far as FedEx was concerned and they didn't really need to see another presentation showing all of the TV viewing statistics and crowd attendances of Formula 1. They took that for granted. He continued by adding that the reason that they had agreed to see me was very simple. I had struck a chord in my approach when I'd highlighted the business-to-business opportunities that potentially existed for FedEx within both Benetton and Formula 1.

"Too many salespeople use sales tools as a crutch, believing that if they go through them all, they will have delivered a powerful argument"

I really appreciated their openness and desire not to waste either their time, or mine. Instead of the presentation that I had prepared, we sat back and had a three-way conversation that eventually went on for just over an hour and a half. Apart from talking about the type of business-to-business opportunities that would be of interest to them, I asked them a lot of questions about the way in which their company operated and we discussed some of the issues facing them in Europe as opposed to the US, where FedEx had become a name synonymous with parcel and letter delivery. At the end of the meeting, I asked them which had been the main areas of interest. They were totally up-front and told me what they could see working and also where they could see problems that would have to be overcome if we were to move forward. I just wish more businesspeople were a little more like these two. They respected my time and I respected theirs. None of us wanted to play games. That meeting was at the beginning of February and after some really hard and protracted negotiations, at both the global headquarters of FedEx in Memphis and at the Benetton F1 HQ in Oxfordshire, the deal was signed in time for the distinctive FedEx branding to appear on the Benetton F1 cars at the British Grand Prix in July.

The whole point about that story is that if I had persevered with my original plan of running through the presentation, I might well have bored both men rigid and quite likely missed the opportunity to develop the areas of the programme that were important to them. It was an important lesson for me; one that I recommend you all to take on board.

SUMMARY

When you approach a company for sponsorship you need to convince yourself that the company will benefit from participation. If you are not convinced, how can you expect the company personnel to be convinced? Sales tools can be very effective in supporting your presentation but you must use them sparingly. Don't feel that because you have taken a lot of trouble to put together sales tools such as PowerPoint presentations, brochures and press cuttings portfolios that you have to use them. They should be there to support you. You need to bring them in and out of play to suit your dialogue, not the other way around.

Loss leader selling

Having raced professionally in South Africa for several years, I finally decided to call it a day at the end of 1987. My last race, for which I had secured the sponsorship deals covered earlier, happened to be the last major international event on the original Kyalami Grand Prix Circuit. The circuit had boasted the longest straight in Formula 1 and was one of the most popular GP tracks amongst the drivers, being both fast and challenging. It also encouraged overtaking. Sadly, there is no South African Grand Prix today. A combination of the South African exchange rate, politics and the cost of bringing the circuit up to modern F1 requirements make the chance of it happening again very slim indeed.

Prior to my retirement, I had been contracted as a race driver to Mercedes Benz in South Africa. Strangely, this involved racing for the Honda works team in what was then the South African equivalent of the British Touring Car Championship. There was a very simple reason for this. Until about 2001, Mercedes built Honda cars in South Africa and if you wanted to buy one, you visited your local Mercedes dealership. It was a unique situation, but one that worked extremely well for both companies.

I was delighted to be able to bring some success to Honda, winning several races as well as the Class Championship. My most satisfying success, however, was in the prestigious 6-Hour Endurance Race at the Killarney Circuit in Cape Town. There were many famous names in that race, including a German F1 driver who had raced for McLaren in Formula 1, Jochen Mass. After he left McLaren, he went on to become the World Sportscar Champion, driving for the Rothmans Porsche team. At that time, Jochen was married to a well-known South African, who had been an international model, and they lived fairly close to me in Cape Town. He had been contracted to race for VW in a few high-profile events in South Africa.

I was privileged to race against Jochen a second time, when I competed in that last race at Kyalami. He was in one of the unbelievably quick Rothmans Porsches. Along with the late Ferrari F1 driver, Michele Alboretto – who I got to know well when he raced for Lola F1 at the time I was involved with the team – Jochen Mass is one of the most genuine people that I have met in the sport. You always got the feeling with both of them that they would have raced for nothing, because it was the racing, not the money, that meant the most to them.

Having informed Mercedes Benz that I was going to retire from driving, I sat down with their marketing director to discuss my options. He came up with what seemed an interesting opportunity.

I was offered the chance to become sales director of a new type of dealership that Mercedes were planning in South Africa, called Silverline, which would specialise in the exotic car market. It was designed to allow Mercedes SA to secure business in a market that was being dominated by the many private exotic car businesses in South Africa. Not only would I get a top-of-the-range car, in addition to a good salary, but so would my wife, Liz. I decided to give it a try. The dealership would operate in Sandton, the elite northern suburb of Johannesburg, where there was plenty of money about and where exotic cars were a real status symbol.

Eight weeks after starting, I drove home one evening and told Liz that we would have to take the cars back. I had quit. I have to say that she wasn't surprised. It had become obvious that I hated the job. Well, not so much the job, but the people that I was working with. It was expected of all the staff to join the dealer principal in the company bar most evenings, where it was also expected that you would laugh at his jokes. I have to say that I really couldn't stand the cronyism that was so evident. I knew that it wasn't going to change, so I had two choices. Live with it or leave. It wasn't a difficult decision to reach.

That evening, as we sat by the pool with the mandatory glass of wine, Liz, not unreasonably, asked me what we were going to do to bring in some money. Even she was surprised when I told her that together we were going to start South Africa's first ever racing driver school.

Just over two months later, Speed International was launched at the Zwartkops Raceway, south of Pretoria. The way that I managed to fund it, not having a great deal of spare cash, will probably not come as a surprise to you. Sponsorship. And lots of it!

"Supermarkets sell some products at a loss to get you into the store. Once inside, it is intended that you'll spend a lot more on profitable items"

The method that I used to secure enough sponsorship, allows me to outline another effective strategy that I have used more than once with great success. I've never really given it a name before, but perhaps I should call it my "loss leader" sales strategy. It's a method of securing sponsorship that is particularly effective for sponsorship properties that are not particularly high profile. It works very much along the lines used by supermarkets, that I'm sure most of you will be familiar with. They will deliberately sell some products at a loss to get you into the store. Once inside, of course, it is intended that you'll spend a lot more on profitable items. This method worked exceptionally well in enabling me to secure a substantial amount of sponsorship for the racing school. As there had never been such a school in South Africa before, there was no way that it could be considered high profile, hence the need for some creative thinking.

Having negotiated a deal with a wealthy businessman who owned the Zwartkops circuit, a sort of South African version of Lydden Hill, I was able to put together a reasonable agreement with Toyota which would provide me with some Toyota Conquest 16 valve cars on loan, fitted with roll cages, seat harnesses and other racing equipment.

As the concept of such a school was new to the country, I realised that I needed something powerful and innovative to attract people's attention and get them to come along to this new business. I came up with the idea of creating a competition at the school, designed to identify the top pupil. What I needed was a prize, which would really capture the imagination of the South

African public. As with any racing school, you cannot survive purely on the business that you might derive from young drivers who wanted to become professional racing drivers. The school had to offer a wider appeal. I still also needed a substantial amount of sponsorship.

I decided to use this school competition as the means to secure a major sponsor, one that would make everyone sit up and take notice. It was very difficult at that time for South Africans to travel to Europe, particularly to compete in any motorsport activities, due to the poor exchange rate of the Rand. I knew that if I could put together a prize which involved a trip to Europe and which included some motorsport activity while there, I would be on to a winner. I then developed a sponsorship sales strategy around this idea.

As I mentioned, what I needed was a sponsor that would create an impact. Had Andre van der Westhuizen Panel Beaters (an imaginary company), for example, given me the money that I required, it would have added absolutely nothing to the credibility or profile of my new school. On the other hand, there was a company operating in South Africa that would.

I had set my sights on RJ Reynolds, the American tobacco giant. The brand that really interested me was Camel. At that time they were big sponsors in Formula 1, as well as being involved in several other motorsport categories. I knew that if I could bring them on board as a major sponsor, it would create just the sort of impression that I was looking for. My first step was to secure a meeting with Peter Buckley, who was the SA marketing manager for RJ Reynolds.

I decided to initiate this by means of a phone call. The main point was to get his agreement that it wasn't easy for Camel in South Africa to derive mileage from the company's international motorsport activities. I then went on to explain that I was launching a brand new motorsport concept in South Africa, one that would undoubtedly generate a high degree of media interest and which could provide a link to Camel's international programme. I asked him if I could come and present this to him.

His response was simple. He told me that he did not have any available budget for that year or the next, and that I was wasting my time as well as his. My response was to ask him if the concept that I had very briefly outlined appealed, forgetting the cost. He agreed that it had merit. I then explained that there was a way in which this could work for Camel with hardly any costs being involved. He was highly sceptical, but agreed to see me.

What I presented to Peter at that meeting was an opportunity for Camel to sponsor the annual competition at the school. I proposed that it should be called the Camel Rookie of the Year Challenge. I have to say that Peter was quite impressed at this. He still insisted that there was one problem, however. He realised that I would want a sponsorship fee from Camel in return for them becoming the title sponsor of the Rookie of the Year programme and he did not have a budget available, having committed most of it to the Camel Challenge, a Range Rover trek across Africa.

This is where I took a calculated gamble. I surprised Peter by telling him that I didn't need a sponsorship fee. I then listed what I wanted his company to supply in return for the title sponsorship:
• One return air ticket to the UK for the Camel Rookie of the Year
• A test day for the Camel Rookie with the Paul Stewart FF2000 racing team in the UK
  (This team was run by Jackie Stewart's son, Paul)
• 500 Camel T-shirts and caps for the school
• The services of his PR Agency to help promote the competition.

I also explained to Peter Buckley that I had arranged with John Kirkpatrick, the owner of the famous Jim Russell Racing Driver School at Donington Park, to provide a week's course for the Camel Rookie winner. This would include a race in a Formula Ford at the end of the course. In return, I had agreed to fly John to South Africa to be one of the judges in the final of the Camel Rookie of the Year competition.

The Camel sponsorship that Brian negotiated for the racing school's Rookie of the Year Challenge, brought very little funding but enabled him to secure a number of other major sponsorships as a direct result of the credibility that Camel added

Peter thought it over for a few days and then told me that we had a deal. The Camel Rookie of the Year was on the road!

There was still a problem, however. Impressive as the name Camel was, it didn't pay for all of the other considerable expenses involved in setting up and running a racing school. These included the design and printing of brochures, track hire, vehicle maintenance, tyres, fuel, helmets and all of the many other major expenses. I wasn't too worried, however, as I had achieved exactly what I had set out to do.

I knew that if I could secure Camel sponsorship for the new Rookie of the Year competition, the high level of credibility that it would give the school would provide me with a superb platform on which to build a range of other sponsorship programmes. I was correct in my assumption. In addition, every pupil coming to the school would get a free T-shirt and cap, branded with the famous Camel badge. In South Africa, that alone was quite an attractive draw-card.

Within two months of the Camel deal being agreed, I had negotiated a number of meaningful deals, including one with an airline, Luxavia, which provided me with free first class air travel. This would mean that not only could Liz and I accompany the Camel Rookie of the Year to the UK, but that John Kirkpatrick's return ticket to South Africa was paid for.

Other deals included a year's supply of petrol for the School from Sasol, tyres from Continental, batteries from Sabat, helmets and overalls from Autoquip. There were many more. I even negotiated sponsorship from Safari Plan, a company that owned exclusive wild game farms close to the Mozambique border with South Africa. This allowed us to spend a few days of rest and relaxation in the African bush whenever we needed it!

All of this was made possible by one thing: the Camel brand name.

You will hopefully see why I called it "loss leader" selling. By realising the power that the Camel brand would provide to my new business, I was prepared to sell the deal at a virtual loss. It's a useful strategy in the right circumstances.

That isn't the end of the story. All of the deals that I was able to put together, which came about as a result of that Camel agreement, probably covered about 50 per cent of my running costs for the first year. It didn't cover such expenditure as instructor fees. Neither did it provide me with a salary. I still needed a major sponsor for the school, one that would pay a sizeable sponsorship fee, as opposed to all the other deals, which provided products or services as payment. Such a cash injection would allow me to move forward with my plans to expand the school.

This is where, once again, I must stress the incredible power of the media when seeking sponsorship. Because the competition had the name Camel attached to it, everyone assumed that they had put in a lot of money. You now know that they didn't. There was another bonus, however, on which I had based my thinking. I knew that with Camel spending a lot of money in South Africa on media advertising, I should be able to secure a worthwhile response from the media in terms of promoting and covering the Rookie of the Year challenge. I was confident that this in turn would help me secure a major title sponsor for the school itself.

I had no idea just how much interest there would be. Within a short space of time after announcing the Camel sponsorship, I was able to arrange no less than four major TV features, as well as a number of radio programmes and magazine and newspaper articles. Having gained agreement with the TV programmes, I knew that before these were filmed, I would have to move very quickly to be able to offer a potential title sponsor the opportunity that this media coverage would present.

Through reading the business pages of the main papers, I heard that a well-known company was about to re-brand itself. PG Windscreens was a very successful company, with a chain of retail outlets across the country. It was about to change its corporate identity and name to AutoGlass.

You may recall that they went on to sponsor the Leyton House Formula 1 team in later years. I approached the managing director of the company and was able to show him how he could achieve a very high media profile for the new brand by becoming the title sponsor of the racing school and thereby enjoying the guaranteed media attention that I had already put in place. It would also provide the company with a superb corporate entertaining opportunity, as it would have the right to book the school for its exclusive use on race days.

In addition to all of these benefits, there was another. I had negotiated a deal with the newly revamped Kyalami Grand Prix circuit, which would mean that I'd move Speed International there. I was able to secure an agreement with the owners that they would allocate a prestigious corporate suite to AutoGlass, as part of the deal. Although the South African F1 Grand Prix was no longer on the calendar, it would provide AutoGlass with an excellent facility for all national race meetings.

"The media coverage that the school received in that first year of the sponsorship programme was quite exceptional"

I had done enough to generate interest. He referred me to his marketing director Louis Rosseau, who was fortunately a man with considerable marketing vision. Within a very short time, I was able to bring the negotiations with the company to a successful conclusion, securing a three-year sponsorship agreement, which was worth a lot of money. The media coverage that the school received in that first year of the sponsorship programme was quite exceptional and the response from all of our sponsors was fantastic.

All of this had come about because I was able to see the value of bringing a high profile brand name to the party, even though it really didn't provide me with a penny. Had I been greedy, I could have lost everything. Although I certainly wouldn't recommend that you go around offering free sponsorship to all and sundry, the careful and occasional use of this ploy can work very well. If you are seeking sponsorship for a property that doesn't have a high profile, this can be a very effective way of overcoming that problem.

SUMMARY

If you have a sponsorship property that is not well known, or high profile, it can be quite difficult to capture the interest of a major brand or company.

If you are seeking several sponsors for your opportunity, it can be very advantageous to attract a well-known company as a sponsor. This will add a high degree of credibility to your sponsorship opportunity. It might also provide the potential for business-to-business dealings for companies keen to be associated with that major brand or company.

By adopting a "loss leader" approach to the introduction of such a high-profile sponsor, you can attract several other key companies. The perception that is created by announcing a high-profile sponsor can easily outweigh the loss of income that results from providing some sponsorship entitlements virtually for nothing.

You need to be careful in using this method. Only consider it if you are confident that as a result of using a "loss leader" you will attract fee-paying sponsors to provide your full budget. The risk is that if you commit to a programme with the "loss leader" and can't fulfil, you could end up with a legal issue or at best, a lot of egg on your face.

RIAS plc

About RIAS

RIAS is one of this country's leading general insurance intermediaries. Its impressive new corporate head office is situated in Poole, Dorset, where some 650 members of its workforce are employed. Another 350 are based in Northern Ireland. RIAS was established in 1994 and is a 100 per cent subsidiary of Fortis (UK) Ltd. Its name, RIAS, stands for the Retirement Insurance Advisory Service.

The company focuses on the over-50s age profile. Its main lines of business are: home, motor, travel, caravan, legal expenses, personal accident, home and motor breakdown and garden cover. In 2004, the company undertook a major re-branding exercise to increase customer awareness and recognition within its local community.

Case study

RIAS does not have a previous history of any kind of sports sponsorship. The company is growing at the rate of 35 per cent, year on year, to the point where it now employs around 1000 staff in its two geographical sites. The company's managing director, Andrew Marchington, recognised that this growth was creating some exciting new challenges for the company.

These included the need to recruit high quality personnel, in line with its on-going growth, as well as the equally important need to retain and motivate existing personnel. In the catchment area for staff recruitment, there is an extremely competitive situation. With an unemployment rate of less than 2 per cent, it is not easy to attract the quality of people that RIAS require. In particular, the personnel come from two age groups, 20- to 28-year-olds and over-50s.

In addition to this, it was recognised that there is an on-going need for brand awareness, not only in the region, but nationally. In such a competitive business sector, a high profile brand was seen as being very important.

The Poole Pirates Team competes in the SKY Elite League, which is British speedways' top flight competition, sponsored by SKY TV. The team is currently the most successful in the country, having won all three of speedway's major trophies in 2003/4. This included the Sky Elite League and the sport's two major knockout cup competitions. It enjoys exceptionally large crowds for the sport, ranging from 3,000-6,000 per meeting.

Speedway has increased in popularity at a rapid rate, not only in the UK, but also internationally. The Speedway Grand Prix Championship now comprises rounds in nine countries, including the UK, where it is held annually in the Millennium Stadium, Cardiff, attracting over 45,000 spectators. SKY TV statistics now show that it is their third most watched sport.

The sponsorship

The outcome of the meetings with Poole Pirates promoters, Matt Ford and Mike Golding, was that RIAS decided to become title sponsors of the highly successful Poole Pirates speedway team. There were three primary objectives on which the sponsorship agreement was based:
1. Staff recruitment
2. Staff retention
3. Brand awareness.

Staff recruitment

Because of the difficulties in recruiting staff in the region this was, without doubt, the most important of all the considerations in progressing this sponsorship.

The region has a labour shortage. RIAS is a relatively new company, only having operated for 10 years. It is competing in the recruitment market against many high profile, big name companies that have been in the region a long time. Many of these are well known national financial institutions, which are equally prominent in the region.

RIAS considers itself a labour intensive business, as customers and potential customers in the insurance business need to talk to people. Recruitment is currently and has always been a key issue. It was the company's intention to move RIAS up the list of choices that are available to job-seekers and job-movers in the region. The target age groups for recruitment are 20- to 28-year-olds and over-50s.

Sponsorship of a high profile local sports team seemed a good way of promoting awareness of the company as a high quality employer of people. There are only two choices in the Bournemouth and Poole region that provide a high enough profile. One of these is Bournemouth AFC Football Club, who play in the Coco-Cola Championship, the other is Poole Pirates Speedway Team.

The other alternative was to consider the two south coast Premiership football teams: Southampton and Portsmouth. These were considered to be too far away geographically in respect of hitting the target job market. They were also deemed too expensive.

The deciding factor between the two options within the region came down to the excellent relationship that the Poole Pirates promoters had built with the regional media, particularly The Echo, which is the paper that was considered by RIAS as being exceptionally important from a recruitment advertising point of view. In addition, the coverage received by the club on both regional TV and radio news programmes also helped the decision.

It was decided that Poole Pirates would provide the best route to achieving the objectives in respect of staff recruitment.

Staff retention

The need to motivate and retain existing staff was also seen as a key factor in the decision to use sports sponsorship. This was particularly important if a campaign was to be mounted to recruit new staff.

Part of the deal that the company negotiated with Poole Pirates was that twice a year RIAS would be able to take its entire staff, together with their families, to an Elite League speedway meet. This would include the opportunity to visit the pits, meet the riders and build a unique relationship with the team.

RIS Insurance wanted to use sponsorship in order to attract better quality recruits – and chose a youthful sport like speedway in order to gain brand awareness in a younger audience.

It was considered important in building not only existing staff ties, but in promoting the company to young people. This also provided a benefit to the team in as much that a lot of people who went to speedway for the first time decided that they enjoyed it and returned as paying spectators.

Another way of involving staff is that each week the company provides 20 tickets as a staff incentive to recognise outstanding work effort.

Brand awareness

SKY TV coverage of the Elite League is exceptionally high. It has a wide range of viewer demographics. Many of the TV viewers are people in the 40- to 50-year-old age group, having been fans of the sport since it previous heyday of the 1950s and 1960s. Others are young people who have seen the rapid growth of the sport in the last decade.

As triple champions, it was likely that Poole Pirates would have eight league matches televised live at the home track during the first year of the sponsorship. This would involve a high number of post-race interviews, with the RIAS brand featuring prominently on the interview area backdrop, as well as on the race-bibs of the Poole riders.

Period of agreement

It was decided that an initial two-year agreement would be the most beneficial for both parties. The first year would allow RIAS time to identify the most effective ways in which the sponsorship could be commercially exploited. It would also allow the relationship between the two organisations to develop in a more relaxed way than if it had only been for a one-year period. Another consideration in agreeing a two-year deal was that it would give the target market time to become fully aware of the relationship. It would be unrealistic to expect the full benefits of the programme to be achieved in one short burst of activity.

Measurement

RIAS is aware of the importance of measuring the cost-effectiveness of the sponsorship programme. It is currently putting in place methods of assessing the number of people who make contact with the company through its call centres as a result of the Poole Pirates sponsorship activities and promotions.

In respect of the primary objective, incoming correspondence from job-seekers is monitored carefully. In June of this year, 17 new employees resulted from unsolicited letters expressing a desire to work for RIAS, as opposed to people responding to advertisements for specific jobs. Before the Poole Pirates sponsorship, this averaged one or two at most.

This has immediately saved the company the normal cost of advertising, which has amortised at £2,000 per application. In June alone, this effectively saved the company over £34,000.

In terms of staff retention, 60-70 per cent of the staff turned out for the first speedway meeting to which all the RIAS personnel were invited. In a high number of cases, they brought family with them, further cementing the relationship between RIAS, their staff and the speedway.

All media coverage is being monitored. This will provide RIAS with an indication of the brand awareness that is resulting from the Pirates' success.

Author's comments

RIAS has shown that sports sponsorship can provide yet another cost-effective benefit. The need to recruit high quality personnel in a highly competitive labour market is a vital requirement for the company. Through an innovative link-up with the region's most successful sports team, Poole Pirates, RIAS is demonstrating that sports sponsorship can play an important role in achieving this objective.

This case study shows the importance of fully understanding and appreciating what is important to a company and not making assumptions. The choice of a speedway team as the sponsorship vehicle for a company that targets the over-50s age group, might at first seem strange. However, as you can now see, this is a well thought out sponsorship programme, based on sound research, vision and an in-depth knowledge of its target market. It is already demonstrating that it is going to be successful in producing the required results.

Getting **a meeting**

Once you've reached the stage where you have developed your sales strategy, you know which companies you are going to approach and you have done your research, there comes that horrible moment of truth. You must now draw a line under your preparation and start the real business of making contact with the decision-makers, with the objective of setting up meetings. I'm sure that there are few of you who would disagree that one of the most difficult aspects of sponsorship seeking is to establish a meeting at an appropriate level within a company. Some of you might even add that it is becoming equally difficult to even get to speak to that person on the phone, let alone arrange a meeting.

There are no hard and fast rules for being successful at this. A great deal depends on what you feel most comfortable doing and on what you find works best for you.

I know that there will be many of you who really hate using the telephone to try to get that important first meeting. Don't worry about it. If you hate what you do, the chances are that you won't be very good at doing it, as in so many walks of life. It's all very well being told that if you practice often enough, you'll eventually become good. It has to be accepted that some people just do not have a telephone voice or manner that works for them. Short of engaging in some in very in-depth training, that is not going to change. If you feel more comfortable making contact with a company by another means, then work really hard at that and spend time creating effective variations which provide you with the best chance of being successful.

If you're not going to use the phone to secure that important first meeting, then it is quite probable that you will choose to make contact with the person in question by means of a letter, accompanied by some sort of presentation or brochure. Whilst I am certainly not a believer in indiscriminate mail shots as an effective way of seeking sponsorship, I know that a personally tailored written approach to a company does work for some people. If you're going to take this route, there are some important points to remember.

As with any approach, the golden rule is that your sole objective should be to secure a meeting, not to try and sell the sponsorship in one step.

Unfortunately, you face one serious problem when you send in a sponsorship proposal in this way. If it is too detailed, the

Rugby Union's growing appeal stems from increased television coverage. But don't forget the audience that it also provides – hardy, passionate people who brave less that perfect condisions to see it.

chances are that a decision will be reached by the marketing personnel, purely based on this, without even speaking to you. They will look through it quickly and unless something grabs their attention straightway, they will put it in a pile along with all the others that will generate an "I regret" response. On the other hand, however, if you don't provide enough information to arouse their curiosity, you're communication will more than likely generate a similar response. What you need is a very fine balance between the two.

Remember, your objective is to establish a meeting, or at worst a phone conversation. It is not to try and sell the whole concept in one go. When you send a letter, it will help greatly if you can discover who is most likely to open it within the company. I have found that in most companies it is the secretary who opens the mail and then sorts it into three piles:
• Worth her boss reading
• Not worth her boss reading, but worth passing on to someone else
• For the bin

This makes your task even more difficult. What you need to ask yourself is; what can you do to make sure that the secretary cannot afford to put your communication onto that final pile?

It's not that she is being obstructive. I find that most secretaries are very helpful if approached in the right manner. The problem is that the moment the word "sponsorship" is spotted, mentally she may already be starting to put it into that final pile. She could have heard her boss tell colleagues that the sponsorship budget has already been used up, or he might have specifically told her not to bother him with any sponsorship proposals for a while. She is only doing her job and there are far more important things for her boss to worry about than yet another sponsorship proposal. It also often happens that if she doesn't recognise the letter as coming from a high profile club, association or even individual, she will at best put it into the "pass-on" pile. That can mean that it sits on someone's desk for the next few weeks and nothing happens. Call me cynical if you like, but I know that this is true.

What might stop her in her tracks?
Well, there is one thing for sure. A letter that offers her company what seems to be a genuine

business opportunity. If the letter gives the impression that you are looking for the company to give you money, however you might phrase it, it won't receive a high degree of interest. If, however, the letter starts by outlining an opportunity for the company to secure some business, there will be a reluctance to take the decision that this isn't likely to be of interest to her boss. Here is a hypothetical example of an initial sponsorship approach to a large wine distributor:

For the attention of Mr Ken Walston,
EURO WINES Ltd

Dear Mr Walston,
Last year, the Top Man Sportscar Team spent in excess of £120,000 on wine for its hospitality facility, which it operates at each Round of the European Sportscar Championship. The hospitality is provided to representatives of the international media, to senior business executives from the teams' sponsors and to a wide range of business people who are invited by the team and its many sponsors.

I would very much appreciate the opportunity to meet with you to discuss an opportunity for your company to be the supplier of this wine requirement for next season. In addition, there is an innovative opportunity for you to set up a product sampling and promotional facility at each of the Rounds, which take place in the UK, France, Belgium, Italy and Germany.

You will find enclosed some background information on the team, which also illustrates our superb hospitality facilities.

I look forward to meeting with you and discussing in more detail the business opportunities that are available to your company.

Kind regards, etc, etc.

I want to stress that you are not in any way misleading the company. The basis of a letter of this type must be factual and totally genuine:
Fact: The Team does spend that amount on wine for its hospitality facility.
Fact: There is an opportunity for the EURO WINE Company to secure this business.
Fact: It would be possible to arrange sampling and promotional opportunities.

It is also a fact that you want to present EURO WINES with the opportunity to become a team sponsor and enjoy a range of benefits that can be derived from that.

The business opportunity will be dependent on a sponsorship deal being agreed. However, you have highlighted the opportunity to do business and hopefully whetted their appetite to find out more. Any marketing person worth their salt will realise that you are not presenting this opportunity out of the goodness of your heart. They expect there to be a "price" to pay.

Obviously not every sponsorship seeker is able to provide such a clear-cut business opportunity, but the principle applies in most cases. You need to be creative and in the opening of your letter, present a strong business reason for them to at least want to find out more.

I learned a valuable lesson about writing sales letters, early on in my business career. In any letter that you send out, the least used word should be "I" and the most used should be "you" or a reference to the recipient's company. If you try to remember this, you'll avoid sending out what I always call the 'gimme' letter. In an extreme form, the 'gimme' letter can best be compared to young children writing to Father Christmas, conveying a list of all the presents that they would like to receive.

Here's a short example of what I mean. You might think this approach is somewhat simplistic and of course, it is – but it is very much in the mould of so many of the letters that I am shown.

Dear Mr Smith,

Last year I won the Formula Ford regional championship. I was also voted the best young driver in the championship. I am keen to progress my career by moving into Formula 3 next season. I have been offered a drive with the Radstock Formula 3 Team, considered the best team in the Championship.

I would like to offer your company the chance to sponsor my car. You will get a great deal of publicity in this way, as the Championship is shown on Channel 4.

I need to have a sponsor in place by the end of December, to be able to confirm my drive for next season with the team.

I have enclosed a video showing footage of my races this season and also a drawing of what the car will look like with your name on.

I hope that you find this of interest.

Yours sincerely, etc, etc.

"What might seem funny to you might be either irritating or even offensive to the person to whom you are sending it"

If you count the number of "I"s and compare it the number of "you"s, you'll see what I mean. As I pointed out, although they may contain a lot more information, there are hundreds of letters that are similar in style to this being sent out every week to potential sponsors. I know that for a fact, because I have asked a number of companies to comment on the standard of sponsorship letters and proposals that they receive.

What else might prove a very powerful reason for the secretary to make sure that your letter is seen by her boss? This is where one of the innovative sales tools that we looked at earlier might come in useful. The bar of Kit Kat that I talked about earlier on is a very good example, just make sure that you don't send something like this in the middle of a hot summer or you could undo any good effect that it might have had if it arrives a soggy chocolate mess. Always make sure that if you send anything, it should be in good taste – and, importantly, remember that what might seem funny to you might be either irritating or even offensive to the person to whom you are sending it.

I don't care how long you've been in the business, or how successful you have been, there are still times when you pick up the phone and it feels as though it weighs a tonne! I quite enjoy what is known in selling terms as cold calling. In fact, one of the biggest deals that I have ever done, taking FedEx to the Benetton F1 Team, started with a "cold" phone call. I must admit, however, that I often get a complete mental block and really have to force myself to pick up the phone to initiate a call when I'm selling a sponsorship property.

Earlier on, I expressed the view that I prefer to see people choose the way of making their initial sales contact, that best suits them. I know that there are many of you out there who feel that you just don't come across well on the telephone. Don't panic. It's not the end of the world. I'm sure that there will be lots of you will quite openly admit that they couldn't write a letter to Father Christmas, let alone to the marketing director of a large company. I understand your problem and sympathise with you.

I am not saying that you shouldn't try to improve these various skills. You should make the effort because it will help you greatly in your future business dealings if you can do that. However, in the meantime, I believe that there are many more ways of skinning that proverbial cat.

I'm sure you will agree with me that you don't stand a chance of securing a deal if you can't establish communication with the person who will make the decision about whether or not to pursue your sponsorship proposals. That communication can initially either be verbal, telephonic, written or electronic. What is important with any of these methods is that you are able to grab the person's attention early on and create a desire in that person to want to know more. The idea of sending a packet of grass seeds was an example that I provided of innovative thinking to gain interest. You need to work on whatever method you feel most happy with. You must make an effort to be original and to show the person whom you are contacting that you are not just thinking of yourself, but are interested in what they might get out of the opportunity. Only in this way will you stand a chance of securing a meeting. As with so much of the selling process, there is no simple right or wrong way. It's what works for you. If it gets you a meeting, it works. If it doesn't, you will have a problem. It's as simple as that.

"If your letter doesn't grab the reader's interest within the first few lines, the chances are that it will go in the 'no thank you' pile"

In considering the best route to take, it may be helpful to look at the pluses and minuses of each method of approach.

Letter

If you don't feel confident about using the phone, writing a letter is an obvious option for you. A well-written letter to the correct person might just create the spark of interest that is all you need to be invited to present your opportunity in more detail. However, I want to emphasise the words "well-written". If your letter doesn't grab the reader's interest within the first few lines, the chances are that it will go in the "no thank you" pile.

I also want to stress the importance of addressing it to the right person. This is where good research comes in. Don't bother sending letters that aren't addressed to a specific person within a company. Quite frankly, you will be wasting your time. Get a name and get the spelling right, as well as the person's initials and title.

It is quite possible that your letter is accompanied by a sales presentation of some sort, or even one of the innovative sales tools that we looked at. Unless you feel really confident that you can write a persuasive letter, I would strongly suggest that you either enlist the help of someone who can or that you book yourself on a business-letter writing course. There are several available. One particular company that I can recommend in this respect is Spearhead Training. Believe me, it is money well spent.

Your letter should be fairly brief, using bullet-points where possible, as opposed to lengthy paragraphs of text. I can assure you that most business people do not have the time or the will to read through anything that looks as if it might be tedious.

A powerful opening paragraph is essential. The difference between these examples will illustrate my point. These hypothetical letters are written by the marketing manager of a rugby-union association, to a potential sponsor:

Letter 1

Dear Mrs Smith,

Last week I read in Marketing (12.08.04) that your company is launching a new product – a coffee drink in a can that can be heated at its point of use. Having seen how many thousands of spectators face arctic conditions on the terraces of the rugby clubs in our Championship, week in, week out, your product would seem to have great potential.

I would like to suggest that we meet, to discuss ways in which your brand could be promoted in an innovative way through a relationship with this high-profile, televised Championship. This could possibly include the opportunity to sell product at each stadium throughout the season.

Letter 2

Dear Mrs Smith,

I would like to introduce you to the Provincial Rugby Union Championship. This Championship is competed for by 20 Clubs, with the top four teams at the end of the season playing in a knock-out format to determine the winner. Amongst the top clubs playing in this Championship are Reading, Bristol, Manchester and Portsmouth.

I would like to meet with you to discuss how you could become a sponsor of our championship as a way of promoting your new instant-heat coffee product.

In the first example, Mrs Smith's attention is immediately brought to bear on a potential benefit of an involvement with your Championship. It links what is obviously important to her, the new product, with a potential opportunity to promote and even sell product. By setting the scene, a cold day at a rugby match, it is designed to capture her imagination.

Unfortunately, the second example is far more typical of the letters that are sent out to companies all the time, and which so often fail to get the desired response – or any response at all. I would like you to consider which you think is the most likely to get a response and then ask yourself the question "why?"

The problem with letters is that unless you are able to follow-up on the phone within a few days, it is highly likely that you will either get a "Dear John" type of letter in response, or, again, no reaction at all. If you have decided to take the letter writing approach, maybe because you don't like using the phone or would rather articulate all the elements of the proposal on paper, therein lies a problem. How do you follow up?

I would suggest that as much as you don't feel comfortable using the phone to initiate a sales contact, its use in following up your original letter is going to be slightly less daunting. However, if you really have a problem with using the phone for whatever reason, and there are some people who really hate the thing, I have to admit that it is something that I can't really do much about. You are almost certainly going to have to talk to someone on the phone at some stage of the sponsorship process, so I would suggest that you either get someone to help you with this, or alternatively, as I suggested before, you go on a telephone sales course to help overcome some of your fears and problems.

The other rule about letter writing, which I touched on much earlier in the book, is that you don't make spelling or grammatical errors. They display to the prospective sponsor a lack of professionalism and respect. At worst, they can totally irritate someone. Many people will take the view that if you can't be bothered to check your spelling, why should they be bothered to read the epistle?

Emails

Moving on from letters, we come to an increasingly used method of communication, the email. I personally use this quite a lot, in conjunction with the telephone.

I find that more and more people do not like being bombarded with cold phone calls, which I can understand. An introductory email softens the approach and gives the person to whom you are sending it time to prepare themselves for your call. Using this method, I normally introduce myself and briefly outline the reason why I would like to initially arrange a phone conversation with them. There is an obvious inherent danger that they might ultimately choose not take the call when they know in advance why you want to speak to them. That is a risk you take. It puts more importance on creating that powerful attention-grabber and on generating a desire to want to know more. If the person still doesn't want to speak to you after you have emailed them, then you would probably have had a tough job in securing a meeting, even if you had used the phone, instead of email, to initiate the approach.

If you have a website that you are happy to use as a reference point, it's always a good idea to provide a link to this in your introductory email. I should add that if your site is not really up to standard, however, then don't draw attention to the fact by providing the link.

Remember, with emails, your objective should once again be simply to secure a phone discussion or a meeting, not to try and sell the sponsorship.

Phone

The phone is an amazing instrument of communication. However, it does pose a few problems. As I touched on earlier, one of these is that an increasing number of companies, as well as company personnel, are isolating themselves from having to use it. You must have noticed the rise in the number of people who tend to hide behind voice-mails. In good faith you leave a message, but how often is a call ever returned?

It's worth looking at it from their point of view. Can you put yourselves in the shoes of someone working in the marketing department of a company, such as Vodafone. Imagine the number of calls that they receive every day, from people seeking sponsorship for one thing or another. It's perhaps not surprising that they don't want to take them all.

Mind you, before I start getting all teary-eyed about the problems that large companies face in this respect, on the other side of the coin is the fact that we all have to put up with the volumes of unsolicited advertising that they throw at us all day and every day, whether it be in the papers, magazines, direct mail, TV or most annoyingly of all, on the Internet. So don't feel too guilty about approaching these people and badgering them until you do get to speak to a human being. You're not really do anything different to what they do all the time. They are trying to sell their products and services. So are you.

There is another problem with phones. Unless you are able to use video-conferencing facilities, it is impossible to read the body language of the person on the other end of the line, or know how hard they are concentrating on what you are saying. For all you know, whilst holding the phone in one hand and carrying on a conversation with you, they could be writing a love letter with their other hand. You're hardly going to get 100 per cent of their attention in that way.

Unfortunately, there is not a great deal that you can to about this, other than to ensure that you ask a lot of questions. From their answers, you should be able to get a picture of whether they are really listening to you.

There is another issue with using the phone that you need to be aware of: phones are notoriously bad at communicating enthusiasm. If you talk on the phone in the same way as you might have a conversation in the street with a friend, it very often comes across to the person on the other end as being rather toneless. What I mean by this is that when you are face to face with a person, you can usually see emotion in their face. As a result, they don't have to necessarily make the effort with their voice as well. On a phone, you don't have that luxury, so you must try to put emotion into your voice, emphasising changes in tone and pitch to make it interesting.

A very good way of doing this is to record yourself when you make phone calls and then it play back. If you are honest with yourself, you'll probably be quite surprised at how one-tonal and flat you sound. This is an area you can work at quite easily to improve your performance.

"You have to find the method which gives you the most confidence and which makes the best use of the skills that you possess"

Finally, don't forget to thank people when you use the phone. I know I'm repeating myself with this, but it is so important in this business. I am constantly appalled at the phone manners of so many people who phone me to try and sell me something. I'm sure that in most cases they don't mean to sound rude, arrogant or forceful, but that's how they come across. On some occasions, if you're lucky, you get a muttered, 'thanks' which sounds as though it is costing them money to use it, but there is no sincerity in the way they use it.

Put in the effort and practice that is required to make your calls sound interesting, enthusiastic, sincere but relaxed and I promise you that you'll soon see a different reaction from the other person. It might not turn a 'no' into a 'yes', but it makes your calls less fractious and you will be more relaxed as a result.

We've now looked at the three basic means of making contact:
• Letter
• Email
• Phone

There are others, of course, but I would see them as being variations of these three.

I now want to describe to you a way of making contact that over the years has worked extremely well for me. There is no guarantee that it will work for everyone, as we are all very different. As I previously mentioned, you have to find the method which gives you the most confidence and which makes the best use of the skills that you possess. It has taken me a while to perfect my system to the point where it works more often than it fails. So if you are going to try it out, don't expect instant results. It will almost certainly take some time to find out how best to use it to suit your own telephone style.

I put together my first ever sponsorship deal back in 1974. Since then, I have lost count of the number of companies that I must have approached for sponsorship of one kind or another. I suppose it must be well over 1,500, and I'm talking about companies with whom I have at least made contact at a meaningful level. That would make my conversion rate about 27:1. In other words, to secure a sponsorship deal, I need to make contact at least 27 companies. That's an awful lot of "no"s and so if you can come up with a better way of making contact that reduces that ratio, please give me a call. I'm always looking for ways to improve. In the meantime, let me continue to outline my favourite way of making contact with a company. It's a method I use when I find it difficult to make contact with a decision-maker in a company, or else when I need to find out who really does make the decision.

It's incredibly simple and straightforward, so obvious in fact, that it always amazes me that more people don't use it. When you've read through it, many of you will immediately shout out that you're already doing exactly what I am proposing. On the few occasions when I have mentioned it to a colleague, they have done exactly that. It's only when I start to probe a little bit deeper about the way in which they use this method, that I find that they only think they are going about it in the same way. The reality is usually very different.

I suppose that I use this way of making contact in about 50 per cent of my approaches to a company. What I do is to make direct contact with the person who I believe is the best source of knowledge within a company. That person is the PA or secretary. (Before I offend anyone, I want to explain that for literary purposes, I am going to refer to this person as "her", although I do realise that there are many excellent male secretaries and PA's.) Now, I can already hear some of you saying that you always speak to the PA and that by being really polite in asking her to put you through to her boss, you're already using my method. Please bear with me a little longer.

In most medium to large size companies, the decision-makers invariably have a PA. It is almost inevitable that you will speak to her, before you are able to secure a phone conversation or even a meeting with her boss. This is where I go about my task in a different way to many sponsorship seekers. They will usually phone the switchboard and ask for Mr or Mrs Prospect, the decision-maker. If they are lucky, they will be put through to their PA. Polite as they may be to her, their objective will still be the same: to speak to the Prospect. This is where the problem so often starts.

Mr Prospect's PA tells you that he is busy and asks if she can help. At this point, some people will briefly explain that they want to talk to him about a really beneficial sponsorship opportunity and ask when he will be free. Some callers don't even do that, taking the attitude that it's none of her business and telling her that they will call back. Some might ask if it is possible for Mr Prospect to call them.

Knowing that it is increasingly difficult to be put through to senior personnel within a company, when you are phoning for the first time, I will instead take a different tack.

When I call the switchboard of the company, I don't ask to be put through to Mr Prospect. Instead, I ask if I could be put through to his PA, asking for her name at the same time. The chances are that you will be put through to her anyway, but at least you now have her name, which is important for the next step.

Now, put yourself in the shoes of that PA. The phone on your desk rings and you answer it. The caller introduces himself or herself. You don't recognise the name. As with most of the calls that you take, you are now expecting that the caller will ask to speak to Mr Prospect. As your job is to protect him from unwanted calls, you get ready to go into defensive mode.

What you are expecting doesn't happen, however.

Instead of the typical 'Good morning, can I please speak to Mr Prospect?' when you pick up the phone, there is a different approach.

"Am I speaking to Jo Stevens, Mr Prospect's PA?"

Yes, you confirm, rather surprised that the caller knows your name.

"That's good, you're the very person that I wanted to speak to. May I have a couple of minutes of your time, as I would very much appreciate your advice?"

You're now thinking that this isn't going the way that most calls go. You agree to help if you can.

"As PA to the Marketing Director of the XYZ Company, you probably have your finger on the pulse of what goes in the company better than most people."

A little flattered, you smile and make some appropriate non-committal reply.

"When it is convenient, I would like to present what I hope is an interesting marketing opportunity to Mr Prospect, which has sport as its catalyst. At the appropriate time, I would very much like to meet with Mr Prospect, and hopefully yourself, to identify areas of this opportunity that might be of interest to your company. As his PA, you obviously know the best way of presenting this to him. What I would like to suggest is that I send through an initial email to you, rather than Mr Prospect, so that you can gain an insight into the opportunity. I'd then very much appreciate your thoughts on the matter. You might also have some suggestions as to how to fine-

"A PA is often extremely close to their boss from a business point of view. They can prove to be very influential and powerful within an organisation"

tune this to make it even more relevant. At that stage, if you could suggest the best way of presenting this to Mr Prospect it would be really helpful."

What do you think is now going through the PA's mind?

For a start she will probably be quite surprised at your approach. You haven't treated her as an obstacle that has to be somehow be overcome, which unfortunately is a fairly regular occurrence in her capacity. Secondly, you've involved her in the business opportunity that you want to present to Mr Prospect. It's not often that salespeople credit her with having the understanding of what their business opportunities might offer her company.

Thirdly, you have treated her with respect and valued her opinion. Finally, you have shown respect for her boss's time, which is important to her.

It's been my experience that in a high number of cases, if approached in this way, the PA will do whatever she can to help you and bring the opportunity to the attention of her boss. Instead of walking into his office and saying, "I had a salesman on the phone who is looking for sponsorship for his motor racing. We're not interested are we?", something that happens only too often, she might approach it in a different way.

What you want her to say is somehting like: "I've been in discussion with a person who contacted me a couple of days ago with what looks like an interesting sponsorship proposal. It would give us the opportunity to perhaps launch our new product at a major sports exhibition that's taking place at the NEC in January. I asked him to send the information through to me, which he did, and I think it might be worthwhile you talking to him. Here's the communication that he sent in, which I've marked up with a couple of other points that he added at my suggestion. Shall I set up a provisional meeting with him for you?"

I'm not saying that every PA will be as helpful as that, but over the years I have been amazed at just how many will be. It depends on your sincerity. If you come across as a bit of a Del Boy, then you're not going to get very far, but if you genuinely treat her as being important within the decision-making process, it will hopefully come across to her. The relationship between a PA and her boss is very often extremely close from a business point of view. If she is on your side, she can prove to be very influential and powerful within an organisation.

Very often, if I don't get any joy within an organisation and can't even get to speak to the marketing or the sales director's PA, I will go right to the very top and ask to speak to the CEO's PA. By adopting a similar approach, I'll encourage her to suggest to whom I should be talking within the company. She then might tell me that the person who handles this is Mr Brown, the communications director.

My next step is to ask her who Mr Brown's PA is? Having found out this name, I will ask the CEO's PA if it would be possible for her to contact Mr Brown's PA and explain that we have had a conversation, adding that I will be phoning her to arrange a meeting. I usually find that if the CEO's PA, at the top of the secretarial hierarchy, contacts another in this way, it will add great weight to your subsequent phone call.

The network of PA's in a company can be very helpful to you if you learn how to work it to your advantage and go about it in a professional, not a "jack the lad", way.

When you do this, it always pays to go back to the people who have helped you progress matters in this way and thank them, informing them of progress.

This might all seem a long-winded way of establishing a meeting, but I can assure you that it has worked for me so many times, that it has to have something going for it. In companies ranging

"Do not try to sell the sponsorship over the phone. You should whet the appetite enough so that they are happy to meet and find out more"

from FedEx to Gillette and from Marconi to AutoGlass, the help that I have had from PA's has played a vital role in my success.

Interestingly, when I concluded the deal with Gillette that saw them become a sponsor of the Benetton F1 team, I received a lot of assistance from the secretary to the President of Gillette, Europe. Her name was Barbara Gel and she has recently retired. I took her out to lunch one day and she told me that she had worked for no less than sixteen Presidents of that company in her working life. No wonder she knew her way around that company better than just about anyone else. She also told me that I was one of the very few sponsorship sales people who had made any effort to involve her in the process and she thanked me for that. Amazing!

Follow up
Whichever route you've gone done when making contact, the next step has to be a follow-up to hopefully arrange that much sought-after meeting. Unfortunately, for those of you who don't particularly like using the phone, this is another part of the job in which use of the telephone is almost mandatory.

One of the reasons why I like to involve a PA in my approach to a company is that it provides you with a point of contact to go back to if you feel you are not making any progress. On many an occasion, I have phoned the PA with whom I started the process and she has done the chasing up on my behalf. That doesn't always mean that it will be good news, however. She will often tell you that the answer is no, but even that is better than simply sitting waiting for a letter or a phone call that never comes.

If you've written a letter to the company, or sent an email, you will obviously need to follow up with the person to whom it was addressed. That may well mean that you are put through to their PA. If you are, remember that she probably receives a couple of dozen letters, minimum, per day, so don't expect her to remember your name.

When she answers, tell her your name, the date on which you sent the letter and a very brief outline of what is was about. You then need to ask her if she knows whether it has yet been read by the person concerned. If it has, you need to get to speak to that person. If it hasn't, you must ask her when you should call again.

Assuming that you get put through to the right person, if you don't expect a particularly communicative response when they take the call, you probably won't be disappointed. The onus will be very much on you to take the lead.

Before we get to the conversation, as I've pointed out many times to you, do not try to sell the sponsorship over the phone.

If you do, the chances are that you'll receive a negative response. What you should be doing is to whet the appetite of the person enough so that they are happy to meet with to find out more. I know that this isn't an easy thing to do. In fact, it's very tough.

When you are eventually put through to the person you asked for, it's natural to want to include as many of the potential benefits as possible in the short time that you are going to be given on the phone. You plough ahead, hoping that one of them might just hit the right spot. Soon, you have

"I choose to be upfront about cost, but only to a certain degree – I am still only trying to secure that meeting, not do a deal over the phone"

no cards left up your sleeve and so the decision will probably be made over the phone, without ever getting a meeting. If it is, it probably won't go in your favour. Don't give out all of the information over the phone. So how do you progress the call?

The first guideline is to avoid asking direct questions, which can be answered with a "yes" or "no", such as: "Did you find the sponsorship opportunity outline that I sent you interesting?"

Rather ask a question which requires some input. These usually start with "how, why, what, where, which, when?" These could be:

"Which features of the outline that I sent through to you particularly appealed?"

"When would be a good time to get together to look at the options in more detail?"

"How would you feel about the potential interest from the education sector?"

Though it is possible to come up with a blunt and negative response to this type of question, it is far less likely. The intention is to get the prospect to open up and provide you with an insight into their requirements.

It is very likely that if you do get the conversation moving along, you will at some stage be asked the question: "How much are we talking about, cost wise?"

Opinions differ on what your response should be. Do you avoid giving out this information or should you be totally open about it? Much as I would like to give you a straight black and white answer, it's difficult to do so. A lot depends on the sponsorship property that is involved.

Although many people will disagree with me, I personally prefer to be fairly up front with a person, even at this stage, on the basis that it can save me a great deal of time and effort. I would rather know at this time that their budget doesn't stretch to even the lowest cost sponsorship option, than go through a long-winded process, only to find out at the end that they can't afford to be involved. Even then, it could be argued that if I were to enthuse them enough, they might find the money. That's true and there may be a few occasions when I will do that, but only when I am very sure that this could be the case. If it is a specific company that I really want on board, perhaps to put a multi-dimensional strategy together, I will be more flexible.

Most of the time, however, I choose to be upfront about cost, but only to a certain degree. That doesn't mean that I get into a detailed discussion about the fees involved and what entitlements they will get for that fee. I am still only trying to secure that meeting, not do a deal over the phone.

Jonny Wilkinson's excellent performances on the pitch, and England's winning World Cup campaign in 2003, have massively increased the desire amongst sponsors to be a part of rugby's resurgence.

If pushed, what I normally prefer to do is outline the approximate starting point financially for a sponsor. However, I will first explain that as the sponsorship programme will be tailored to suit their identified marketing requirements, it is difficult to put a price on it at this stage until we have selected the range of entitlements that they feel are essential. If they don't have a problem with that and are happy to move on without pushing the point, fine. Nevertheless, they might still insist on a guideline figure, in which case I will tell them what the lowest and highest fees might be.

It is my experience that if a prospect insists in wanting to know the costs, he will get very irritated if you aren't up front with him. It will be assumed that you have something to hide and, in many cases, prospects just can't be bothered to play games, which is how they see it. Tell them the range of fees, but don't go any further than that if you can avoid it.

How do you bring your phone conversation to a successful conclusion? One way is to provide the prospect with some alternative dates when you could arrange a meeting.

"I'm in Chester next week and could be available on either Tuesday or Thursday, or would Monday the 17th be suitable?"

If you come across as though you expect to get a meeting, it will be far better than sounding hesitant and nervous.

You may find that you are asked to provide the person with some more information before they are prepared to arrange a meeting with you. This obviously isn't the ideal scenario as it means that you have lost the advantage of direct communication. You should still try to push for a face-to-face meeting by explaining that you would like to run through that information personally, to avoid any confusion.

If the prospect won't agree to a meeting, however, sending the information does provide you with the chance to continue your discussion at some stage in the next few days. It's better than being told the company isn't interested. Try to agree on a date with the prospect when you will phone him to follow-up on the material that you are sending. Even that is a form of commitment and worth trying to achieve.

In this chapter, we set out to find the most effective ways of making contact with a company. I outlined the method that works best for me, but there are many other ways of achieving the objective of a meeting with the decision-maker. My advice to you is that, within reason, whatever innovative way you can come up with of securing a meeting with the appropriate person, you should go for it. There are no hard and fast rules in this business. In my opinion, if it works for you, it's good. If it doesn't, you have at least tried.

"You need to be prepared to answer questions about the sponsorship fee. Don't try to be devious when replying as it can irritate the prospect"

SUMMARY

There are several ways in which you can make your initial sales approach to a company. These can include:
• Letter
• Email
• Telephone

You need to be honest with yourself as to which methods you are least comfortable with. That doesn't mean that you can't try to improve your skills in those areas. It does mean that whichever method you decide to use, it should be worked on until it is as effective as you can make it.

Whatever method you use, it is important to remember that you are not going to sell the sponsorship at the first attempt. Your objective should be to secure either a meeting or a meaningful telephone conversation with a person at the appropriate level within the company

If you decide that you are going to communicate initially be letter, you will need to create a powerful attention-grabbing opening paragraph:
• Make sure that you don't make spelling and grammatical errors in the letter.
• Always address the letter to an individual.
• If you send emails, make sure they are used only to introduce yourself, prior to a telephone follow up.
• Take as much trouble checking spelling as with a letter.
• Your letter should contain more "you"s than "I"s.

If you use the phone, it is worth practising with a voice recorder to ensure that you speak with the right level of pitch and tone. Enthusiasm and a smile does come across on the phone.

The secretaries in a company can be extremely helpful if you approach them in the right manner. Involve them in what you are trying to achieve and excite them about your sponsorship opportunity. Remember to thank people who have helped you and to inform them of progress.

You need to be prepared to answer questions about the sponsorship fee. Don't try to be devious when replying as it can irritate the prospect. If you have calculated the fee as shown earlier, you have nothing to feel embarrassed about. Remember at all times that you are not trying to sell the sponsorship over the phone, only the idea of a meeting.

Chapter 4

One chance to create a
first impression

I t might come as a surprise when I tell you that in my opinion, you've now covered what are the most difficult steps in the entire marketing strategy. I have always found that the preparation and salesmanship necessary to secure a meeting with the decision-maker is the hardest part of the sponsorship sales process.

Once you are sitting in front of the person you targeted, you've achieved a worthwhile level of success, because if there had been absolutely no interest on their part in considering your sponsorship proposal, you wouldn't be there. It is very rare for people to waste their time going through the motions of a meeting unless they have a reasonably open mind on its possible outcome.

Once you are face-to-face with the person you need to convince, so many advantages come into play. For a start, you can see reaction on the person's face. This makes a huge difference and helps you gauge the impact of what you are putting across. Then there is body language. If you can learn to read body language, in this type of situation, it can prove extremely useful. In some circumstances, you might be able to learn even more about the person you are talking to by looking around their office. You'll be surprised how many senior executives personalise their office, providing you with great opportunities to store this information and use it when appropriate. You might notice several photos of the prospect sailing, or perhaps they have a professional qualification diploma on the wall. This type of information can be very helpful in building a rapport.

Before looking at what happens once you're in that first meeting, it's important to prepare properly for it. What I am going to run through now will seem very basic to many of you. There will be many people, however, who haven't had much experience in this area, so I'm going to look briefly at the guidelines, which might stop you from making some of the mistakes that I know I've been guilty of in the past.

Obvious as it sounds, make sure you know where to go for your meeting. I've arrived at the main entrance of a large company on time, only to find that the marketing department happens to be in a separate building over half a mile away. It was my own fault because I hadn't bothered to confirm beforehand where I should go. As a result, by the time I got to the right office, I was both ten minutes late and certainly far from being relaxed.

Punctuality is important. It shows respect for your prospect's time. There are few acceptable excuses for being late, because most eventualities can be foreseen. Checking out where to park is one of them. Traffic hold-ups are another. You know that there is a good chance of congestion on the roads, so allow for it.

Better to arrive at the address early and pop into a coffee shop, read the paper for a few minutes and relax. In that way, you'll be in the right state of mind.

Dress code for a meeting is a very personal thing and I wouldn't dream of telling people what to wear. However, there is an old, but very well proven, statement that you get one chance to create a first impression. You're there to present a business proposal, so why not look businesslike? You're not there to try to make a fashion statement. That doesn't mean you can't be individual, just remember that you could be meeting people who are a lot older and more formal than yourself. Whatever your style of dress, there is no excuse for dirty shoes.

On the subject of appearance, I have a short beard. I recall having lunch with the President of Gillette after concluding a sizeable F1 sponsorship deal with the shaving division of the company. He told me, with a smile on his face, that I was the first salesperson who had come into his office with a beard, taken a few of million dollars off of him and walked out, still with a beard. Nevertheless, I always make sure my beard is well trimmed!

"Remember, you will almost certainly have asked for the meeting, so the onus is on you as to how it gets started"

What other preparation can you make? You should have already worked out your strategy, based on the research you've done, and so you need to make sure that you've got all of the materials that you need, with copies to leave with the prospect. Make sure you've got business cards with you that are clean and not dog-eared, and a notebook and pen. Don't laugh! You'd be surprised at how many people arrive at a meeting and have to ask for a writing implement.

When you get to the company, it's always worth visiting the cloakroom to check out your appearance. I once interviewed a girl who had a large piece of green vegetable wedged between her front teeth. I found it very distracting and when she later discovered what she had done, she was probably highly embarrassed. If you are really nervous before the meeting, it's a good idea to hold your wrists under a cold tap for a minute or two. It will help cool you down and relax you.

Meeting guidelines

Are there any guidelines relating to the opening minutes of the meeting? Very much so. The first couple of minutes can easily dictate how the rest of the meeting is going to develop. It's important, for example, to appear relaxed when you meet your prospect. That doesn't mean a big cheesy grin, but remember that if your nervousness comes across, it might rub off on the other person. It's always a good idea to thank them for taking the time to meet with you when you first meet them.

The most important thing of all is that you need to take control of the way the meeting starts. Remember, you will almost certainly have asked for the meeting, so the onus is on you as to how it gets started. Don't just sit there waiting for the other person to make the running. It may be that the prospect is keen to put you at ease and will make a few general remarks about the weather, your journey or something of this nature. It's fine to take advantage of this for a brief period, but be careful not to overdo it. Try and bring it round to business as soon as you feel that it's polite to do so. I always rehearse my opening gambit in the car on the way to a meeting. I put together a couple of sentences that often end with a question. I do this so that I can steer the meeting in the direction that I want it to go. A lot of people who you meet will disrupt your plans by asking a difficult question right at the beginning. It can easily throw you, so you have to get in first. What sort of opening do I use? Here are a couple of examples:

"First of all Mrs Smith, thank you for taking the time to meet with me this afternoon. I thought it might be helpful for you if I ran very briefly through the background to the sponsorship opportunity that I would like to present to you, and then we could look in more detail at the areas which you feel could be of particular interest."

Or: "Mr Jones, I very much appreciate the opportunity to discuss with you ways in which one of our championship's events might play a role in promoting the launch of your new brand. It would be really helpful if you could briefly outline your thinking on the targeting of this brand. Where do you see the main interest coming from?'"

What you are doing in both cases is taking control and heading the discussion in the way you want it to go. It will also take away that worry of not knowing how to get the meeting under way.

From this moment on, it becomes quite difficult to guide you through the meeting, because it will vary considerably depending upon the sponsorship property you are selling.

However, there are many points that might help you bring the meeting to a successful conclusion. By successful, I don't necessarily mean that you walk away with a positive decision; it's fairly unusual for that to happen. You should be looking to find out if there are enough potential benefits for the prospect to form the basis of an agreement. In effect, your objective is to find enough common ground that you both consider it worthwhile moving to the next step. That next step might well be a meeting with some other people in the company, or it might be a visit to your premises, if that is appropriate.

One of the best ways to move a meeting along and gather vital information is to ask questions. What you shouldn't do is to bore the poor prospect rigid with a long spiel about how good you are in your particular sport, or to effectively tell him how stupid he would be to turn down such a great opportunity. It is vital to create a situation in which the prospect doesn't feel that he is being sold to, or even told what is going to be good for him. Think how you feel about being told that something is good for you. What is your reaction when you have been feeling a little unwell and a friend or family member insists that they have just the thing that will make you feel better?

"A sore throat, you say? I know exactly what will make you feel better. It's an old recipe that my grandma swore by. Sit down and I'll make some up and bring it over to you."

Well-intentioned as the person may be, you immediately feel a resistance to the solution. Had it been phrased differently, you might have reacted in another way.

" A sore throat, you say? Are you taking anything for it? Would it help if I told you of a remedy that I've been taking for a couple of years now?"

Here is a similar example, but in a business setting: "A new product launch, you say? This sponsorship opportunity that I am offering you is just what you need to create a high level of publicity."

"Really?" So you know more than I do about what I need, mutters the prospect to himself.

Structured in a different way, the response might be more positive: "A new product launch? That's interesting. From what we've discussed so far, which aspects of this sponsorship opportunity do you feel might be helpful in promoting the brand to your target audience?"

The power of carefully worded questions is immense in a selling situation. But there is one cardinal sin that every single one of us makes on far too many occasions, and not only in business. We ask a question, but we don't listen to the answer! Instead, we are too busy thinking of what we are going to say next. By doing so, we make two major mistakes: First, we don't hear what we're being told because we're only listening to half the answer. Second, we fall into the trap of making assumptions in our response. We think we know what the answer to our question is going to be by the time the prospect is halfway through replying and we base our response on that. In many cases we assume wrong!

If you are going to pose questions, you are wasting your time if you don't sit back and listen to what the prospect is telling you. What you should be trying to achieve in this first meeting is to establish a dialogue between yourself and the prospect, not a monologue from either of you. If you go about this in the right way, you can hold a conversation with the other person that makes both of you feel comfortable and relaxed, without stress, knowing that you are simply exploring opportunities, which may or may not be beneficial to their company. You have stopped being a salesperson. What you are doing, in effect, is evaluating through dialogue whether you can be of assistance to that person. There is a distinct difference.

I said that the power of questions is immense. That's true, but only if you go about using them in a strategic manner, as you will see.

When you are meeting that prospect for the first time, what are the underlying principles that will dictate the ultimate acceptance or decline of your proposals?

Put simply, the sales meeting is a conversation between you and another person. The ultimate objective is to reach a conclusion as to whether that person is:
• Satisfied with their current marketing activities and has no desire to add to them, or change them
• Satisfied with their current marketing activities but is prepared to look at other possibilities
• Not satisfied with their current marketing activities and wants to look at ways of improving matters
• Not satisfied with their current marketing activities but doesn'y want to look at other possibilities.

What you have to do is find out which scenario you are facing. You can do this by:
• Asking questions
• Listening to the full answers
• Asking more questions to probe their real feelings about a situation.

You should be looking to determine whether or not there is a need for what you have to offer. That's not all, however. Perhaps even more importantly, you need to find out if there is a genuine desire on the part of your prospect, to identify ways in which your sponsorship property might be able to meet some of his or her marketing needs.

In the next chapter, I am going to introduce a structure for the meeting which can help you move forward, by understanding at any point just where you are in relation to your own objectives.

SUMMARY

You have done well to secure a face-to-face meeting. Make sure that you don't waste the opportunity by not preparing properly. You need to check location, time, and parking and always have a checklist to ensure that you have everything you need with you. Always have an objective in mind for the meeting.

It is important that you lead the way at the meeting. You should not hand over the advantage to the prospect. Before you go to the meeting, prepare an introduction that will steer the meeting in the direction you want. Remember that the more relevant information you can extract from the prospect, the easier your task will be in preparing a proposal based on the company's specific requirements.

Use questions starting with "How, Why, When, What if" to secure this information.

It's no good asking questions if you don't listen to the answers.

Try to gain confirmation from the prospect regarding which entitlements are important to him.

At this first meeting, you need to ascertain whether or not your sponsorship opportunity can really help that company achieve its marketing objectives. If it is obvious that it can't, be honest and gain the respect of the prospect by telling him so. You are not losing a sale by doing this – there probably wasn't a sale to be had in the first place. Your opportunity is not the panacea for the needs of all companies.

SodaStream

About SodaStream

Within the main body of the book, hopefully you will have read about the successful sponsorship agreement that I was able to put together with SodaStream. This was the deal that finally allowed me to fulfil my goal of becoming a professional racing driver – and start my career in sport.

I promised that I would provide you with the details of how this deal was structured. This case study offers an insight into the reasons why SodaStream accepted my proposal. Although this deal took place early in my motorsport career, I feel that it is still as relevant now as it was then, which is why I have included it in the book.

Case Study

When I first came into contact with Don Philpot, the sales manager of SodaStream, the company had just gone through a management buy-out (MBO) from Kenwood. The new company would specialise in the sales of SodaStream dispensing machines and bottles of concentrate. Its product would be sold mainly to retail outlets, including departmental stores, but there would also be wholesale dealers.

The concept involved in the marketing of SodaStream was very similar to the marketing of razors and blades, where the profit comes from sales of blades, not razors. In the same way, SodaStream would make its profit from the sale of concentrate, not from the sale of the machines. Once customers had purchased a machine, the expectation was that they would continue to buy the bottles of concentrate. At that time, a choice of eight or nine flavours was available.

Following a period of research, I was able to identify the major marketing requirements for this new MBO. The main points that were important to the company were:

Brand awareness

This was important now that SodaStream would no longer be advertised and promoted by parent company, Kenwood.

PR

Generation of as much positive media coverage of the newly-independent product and its qualities was an essential part of the marketing mix.

Database generation
The opportunity to communicate special offers and promotions to customers who had purchased the concentrate was seen as being extremely beneficial.

Image transfer
Although it was largely women who purchased SodaStream machines, the decision was influenced by children and young adults. It was important to create a cool, exciting, colourful image for the product.

Sales promotion
Opportunities to promote sales of machines in retail outlets was considered a vital part of the marketing plan. The more machines that were sold, the higher the sales of concentrate.

Product sampling
If people could be persuaded to sample the range of drinks that SodaStream could produce, it would greatly help in encouraging them to purchase.

Staff motivation
Being a new company, there was a need to introduce team-building and incentive programmes to encourage staff motivation and loyalty.

Dealer Incentives
The opportunity to provide wholesale dealers with incentive programmes was considered to be very important to future success.

Merchandising
The opportunity to develop a themed range of SodaStream branded t-shirts and caps would be very helpful in developing brand awareness.

Having identified these as being the main factors that comprised the marketing plan, I needed to put together a proposal that would show how motor racing could help deliver many of these. This had to be in conjunction with some of the more conventional marketing activities such as media advertising and in-store merchandising displays.

The proposal
The creation of an innovative promotion called SodaStream Team Racing. This would have, as its catalyst, the sponsorship by SodaStream of a Formula Ford 1600 racing car, which would compete in the high profile national Townsend Thoresen Championship.

SodaStream Team Racing would encourage the public to take an interest in their racing activities by offering them the chance to become a member of the team. This would be achieved by designing and attaching a collar to every bottle of concentrate that was distributed from the factory. This collar would incorporate an application form, enabling the public to send in their names and addresses, together with a small fee, which would cover postage and packing. In return they would receive:
• An A3 size colour poster of car and driver
• A car sticker
• Free ticket to watch the team race at any of the national tracks such as Brands Hatch, Silverstone and Oulton Park

Special promotional material that appeared with bottles of SodaStream in the early 1980s. It was very successful in driving brand awareness of a new company recently split from its large parent.

- A brochure of Team SodaStream merchandise that could be purchased
- A discount voucher on their next SodaStream purchase
- A competition entry form, the prize for which was the actual race car (at the end of the season) and a course of lessons at a racing driver school.

The programme would be designed to deliver all of the major factors that had been identified as being important to the SodaStream marketing plan.

Brand awareness
- The car would be painted in the distinctive SodaStream colour scheme and livery
- The driver (myself) and pit crew would wear fully SodaStream branded race suit and uniforms
- The car would be ferried in a fully SodaStream branded transporter
- The team would race in the national FF1600 Championship at circuits all over the UK

Database generation
By completing the application on the collars, the public would help to provide SodaStream with a national database.

Image transfer
The racing activities would greatly increase the perception of SodaStream being exciting, cool, colourful, young, daring, extreme and slightly rebellious.

Sales promotion

This was an area in which the motor racing programme really came into its own as a marketing tool, driving growth in the brand. It was proposed that the SodaStream racing car would be made available as a display to major retail outlets, defined by the geographic area in which the team's next race would take place.

The concept was very simple; the car would be prominently on display in the retail outlet. I would be there in a race suit, together with a promotional girl recruited by SodaStream. As the public came into the shop, it was anticipated that many of them would want to look at the race car. If they wished, they could be Polaroid-photographed sitting in the car. While this was happening, other members of their group would be offered free glasses of SodaStream by the demonstrator and told how few pence each one actually cost to produce using the SodaStream machine. There was a special offer for purchase of the machine at the point of sale. This was expected to encourage a lot of mothers with young children in particular.

Dealer incentives

A programme was put in place that would offer target-achieving dealers the chance to bring their families to a race meeting to watch the team in action.

Staff motivation

Group visits to race meetings were organised for the staff.

Merchandising

A range of T-shirts, jackets and caps, branded with the SodaStream Team Racing logo would be produced, which could be ordered by mailorder but also available in SodaStream retail outlets.

PR

Media generating activities that were proposed included launching the team on the pitch at half-time during a Football League Division 2 match at the local stadium, as well as a more formal launch in a top London hotel. It was proposed that the team would then participate in high profile charity events. The racing programme would provide a constant source of news stories. Lifestyle stories were encouraged, based on the personal aspects of the people involved, such as the training regimes of the driver, catering at a race track and similar types of stories.

The result was that SodaStream agreed in full to the proposals that I had made. The success of the programme could be measured fairly accurately through the sales of machines at point of sale in the retail outlets; through the size of the database that was generated, and by the return from sales promotion mailed to team members.

At the end of the year, although the racing hadn't been a spectacular success, due to the reasons outlined in the book, the programme was judged to be a definite by the management team. It was decided to continue with a motor racing programme the following year, but events changed the decision on what this should be.

Comments

Hopefully, this will show you how a programme can be put together which meets the real, not the assumed, marketing requirements of a company. It was only through thorough research that these needs came to light. Once they had been researched and confirmed as being important by the SodaStream management, it was relatively easy to create an imaginative programme that incorporated all of these.

The power of **questions**

It is very tempting at this stage to spend a considerable amount of time looking at the psychology of selling. Psychology plays an important role in the sales process. The interpersonal relationship between a seller and buyer is a fascinating subject. However, there are literally hundreds of books that have been written on the subject, by people far more knowledgeable about it than I am.

Selling has always fascinated me. It isn't just about two business people embroiled in a meeting. Selling is about life. There isn't a day goes by without us having to be a salesperson in some way. Right at the beginning of this book I said that everyone is able to sell. I do mean everyone.

You might want to go out for a drink, so you phone a friend who tells you that he wants to watch a TV programme. You suggest that, as it might be the last fine evening for a while, he should record the programme and come out with you instead. You are selling the idea that going out for a drink on a lovely summer evening is better for him than sitting on the sofa watching TV.

You decide it's time for a pay rise. You meet your boss and put forward your case. That is selling. Selling your sponsorship opportunity to a prospective sponsor is only an extension of what you do every day of your life, whether you realise it or not.

As fascinating a subject as it is, I'm not going to delve into the psychological aspect of selling to someone who is effectively a stranger to you. I would suggest that if you really want to find out more about that aspect of the business, you should go along to your local specialist bookstore or library and choose one of those many books that are available on the subject.

What I would like to look at is the way you can structure a meeting to make it not only more effective, but to ensure that you have the confidence of knowing what you are doing at any one time within that meeting and why you are doing it.

A meeting rarely goes according to plan, however well you have prepared and however much you think that you're in control. The problem is that, although you might know the script inside out, your prospects don't have that privilege. This often results in them not wanting to stick to the sequence that you have planned. Inconsiderate as it may be, they will sometimes even have the temerity to ask a question that will throw you completely off track, because you only wanted to deal with that issue much later in the meeting.

I stressed the importance of being in control, so how could this interruption to the flow of the meeting happen? Imagine a pair of ballroom dancers. The man leads and the woman follows. In that way they achieve their objective of moving around the floor, including the various steps and movements they planned. Imagine if neither took the lead, or even worse, they both tried to take the lead. I think you'd agree that they would have a problem getting started. One of them needs to be in control. It's the same with your meeting. One of you needs to take the lead and it should be you. The difference is that the female dancer knows the routine, albeit led by her partner, whereas the prospect might be quite happy for you to set the pace initially, but he doesn't know the routine and may want to bring up matters that are important to him in a different sequence. You can't control that.

How do you cope with this situation? Too often it will completely throw you and you forget where you were heading and what points you wanted to cover. It can all end in disaster and often does.

You can stay in control of the overall direction of the meeting if you have a strategy which you are following, but which is flexible enough to allow for diversions. It's based on the topic covered in Chapter 16, and focuses on the type of question you should be asking at any stage of the meeting.

When I talk about finding out information through questioning, I don't mean that you should go into the office armed with a long list of questions written down on a sheet of paper, which you then work through in strict order. Think of it more as probing for information. You are looking for the information that will help you assess whether this company has a need, whether it is aware of that need, whether your sponsorship property could help fulfil that need and whether the prospect is receptive to looking at ways in which this might happen.

"A meeting rarely goes to plan. Although you might know the script inside out, your prospects don't have that privilege"

To accommodate for interruptions, changes of direction and the many other situations that can hinder your progress towards these goals, you need to have a structure in place that should be capable of letting you know where you are at any time in relation to the process of probing. When there is an interruption, for whatever reason, you can easily get back on track because you know where you were, where you are right at that moment, and where you want to be.

Probing can be broken down into several stages. We need to identify these stages that will help create what can best be described as a route map for the meeting. It's like planning a journey. You are starting off in Chichester and you want to arrive in Newcastle, so you plot your route. If you hear on the car radio that there is major hold-up on the A1 at Peterborough, you can check your map and take a diversion that will eventually lead you back to the A1, some 20 miles further north. These are the stages that you will go through in the course of a typical sales meeting:

The identification stage
You need to be probing for information that will make it clear where the company is, in a marketing sense, at the present time and where it has come from. It will help you if you can piece together at this stage a picture of how the company operates in reaching marketing decisions.

The needs awareness stage
This is where you are looking for your prospect to tell you whether their current marketing programmes are working. How they could be improved. Are there any problems? What would he

or she like to happen that isn't happening at present? This is when you should be trying to identify what features of your property are benefits and which aren't.

The "What if?" stage

This is the stage in the probing process where you start to put in questions that begin with "What if?" These might include: "What if there was a way of attracting a large number of visitors to your exhibition stand? Would that help increase the sales which you mentioned were not as good as you expected?" Or "What if we could introduce you to the CEO's of our other sponsors with a view to potential business-to-business opportunities. Would that be important to you?" In other words, you are exploring areas of potential benefit to the prospect.

The solution stage

This is the stage where you need to discuss and gauge the reaction of the prospect to what might be the basic foundations of a possible sponsorship agreement. By this point you should have gained a good idea of what will help the potential sponsors achieve their real, not assumed, marketing needs.

"Can we summarise the areas of the proposal that you find particularly interesting?"

"Would I be right in saying that it's the branding opportunity that interests you most about the opportunity?"

The qualification stage

It is at this stage that you need to start finding out whether your prospect is in a position to take action if it is appropriate. Is there a budget? What sort of timing are you looking at? Who needs to be in the decision-making process for this to happen? This is important information because it could save you a great deal of wasted time and effort. If it is clear that there is no budget, you need to know. If three other people need to be involved in the decision-making process, you need to know. If the decision process is going to take five months, you need to know.

The commitment stage

This is the final part of the structure. It is the stage where you have to gain a commitment from the prospect to move forward. It doesn't mean that you necessarily get a decision on the proposal. What you need is a commitment to what you see as being the next important step. Perhaps it is a commitment to put a follow-up meeting in the diary. It may be a commitment to meet with some of his colleagues. It could well be a commitment to allow you to present a personalised presentation, based on the information that has come out of this meeting. Whatever it is, you need to gain that commitment to the next step. A ploy that I often use is to ask the very straightforward question: "Where we do we go from here?" In other words, I put the ball firmly back in the prospect's court. I then do something that doesn't come easily to salespeople. I shut up!

I talked about the power of questions. The power of silence is also very effective. If you ask a question, wait for an answer. It is all too easy to wait for a second or two, but it becomes slightly more difficult to sit there for much longer without feeling embarrassed by the fact that no-one is speaking. Persevere with it. It is surprising what develops if you are prepared to wait.

Too often a salesperson will jump in just as the prospect is quietly considering his response and make some comment that can change the entire direction of the sales process. That critical moment when the prospect could be coming to a positive conclusion is lost. The pressure that you were effectively exerting has been taken off. Putting it bluntly, you need to learn when to shut up.

Ask a leading question and then keep quiet. Don't be the first to speak. The pressure on the other person becomes quite considerable. If you use this tactic sparingly, it can be very powerful:

"Mr Brown, is there any reason why we can't move forward on this?"

"Mrs Black, you've agreed that this opportunity can provide you with a great platform for your marketing activities next year. What's the next step, from your point of view?"

On the subject of keeping quiet, we all know people who talk across you when you are in a conversation. They might ask you a question and mid-way through your answer, they dive in with a comment, or else they show through their body language that they can't wait for you to finish so they can have their say. It's obvious that they aren't listening to what you have to say and are far more interested in their own opinions. It can be very irritating, so don't make that same mistake yourself.

Nearly every question that you are likely to ask within the framework of a sales meeting with a prospect will fit into one of these categories. What you need to do is to continually practice developing an awareness of the reason why you are asking a particular question. Then you should mentally classify it under one of the category headings that I've just outlined. In that way you keep control of the flow of the meeting by knowing just where you are in the logical progress from "identification" to "commitment". You will be able to bring the conversation back to where you want it to be at any stage of this process, should you be taken off-track by a question or opinion that the prospect raises that is out of sequence.

This might seem a rather tedious process, but I have found that it has helped me considerably. It comes back to Michael Schumacher and his ability to win Grands Prix by implementing a smarter strategy than his rivals. He has the ability to be aware at any time during the race just where he is in relation to the planned strategy. If another team disrupts his race by changing its fuel stop strategy, for example, he is still able to adapt to that quickly, because of the fact that he is in control of his own strategy.

In the same way, you should be able to steer your dialogue with the prospect back on course by asking a question from the category where you feel you should be. No matter how many questions he has thrown at you during the period in which you have gone in a different direction, you should still feel confident that you are in control.

SUMMARY

It is important to have a strategy for your meeting, so that you know where you are at any time in respect of your objectives. The use of questions will be far more effective if they fit into a "route-map" so that they always have a purpose. Your questions can be categorised under the following headings:

• Identification
• Needs awareness
• What if?
• Solution
• Qualification
• Commitment.

If you are aware, when you ask questions, as to which category the question falls under, it will help guide you to the final stage which is the commitment from the prospect to the next step in the sales process.

The power of silence can be a very effective way of putting on pressure. You ask a question and then you shut-up until the other person answers.

vodafo

vodafone

The lost art of **listening**

I 've gone on at length about the power of questions. I've also emphasised the need to listen to the answers, but it might come as a surprise to you that I am going to spend some time looking at how you can listen more effectively.

You might wonder how you can learn anything about listening? Surely you just keep your mouth shut and your ears open. What is there to discuss? Well, for a start, you can hear what is being said without taking on board the information that is being communicated to you. Have you ever sat in a room with the radio switched on, broadcasting a programme in which people are involved in a conversation? You want to read the paper and so you start browsing through it. The radio is still on and the conversation is in full swing. However, you become so engrossed in a particular article in the paper, that you effectively close your mind to the sound of voices. Although you heard every word, you didn't actually listen to what was being said.

Think about the conversations that you have in a business sense, or even socially. You ask someone a question. Can you honestly say that you always listen intently to the answer or are you, like most of us, too intent on thinking what your next question is going to be? If you are guilty of that, then you can't be focusing all of your attention on what they are telling you. Similarly, you can ask a question and be so convinced that you know what the answer will be, that you don't really listen to what is being said.

On another occasion, you might ask a question and misunderstand what the answer actually means. This can lead to major problems further down the road in the sales process.

If you don't believe what I am saying, you need only to listen to other peoples' conversations, perhaps on the bus or train. What you will often realise is that there is actually more than one conversation going on. Although both individuals might be asking questions, they are so obviously intent on capping what the other person is saying that they hardly hear the answers.

Asking a question, listening to the answer and responding, not to what you think will be said, but to what has actually been said, is a very difficult skill to acquire. Few of us do it well. However, if you can master the technique, you will notice that not only does the conversation flow more easily and in a far more relaxed style than previously, but also that people will be happy to talk to you because they realise that you are genuinely interested in what they are saying. That is a rare thing to happen, particularly in the selling business.

As I explained, one of the problems that often arises from not listening properly, is that you misunderstand the information that is being fed to you. If you are going to build a strong case for your sponsorship proposals, it must be able to satisfy the needs of the company. If you haven't fully understood what those needs are, as a result of not listening properly, you could find yourself on very thin ice later on. If you are given some detailed information, or perhaps a complex opinion on a subject, by your prospect, you need to be sure that you understand not only what they are saying, but also what they mean. You can achieve this by repeating the information that they volunteered, preceded by the words: "If I understand correctly, what you are saying is that…" or "Can I just run through that again with you, to make sure I fully understand what you are saying?"

Provided that you don't do this too often, you will not only have a better picture of what you are being told, but you will also gain the respect of the other person. They will feel that you are actually listening to them and not simply going through the motions of listening.

The whole point about asking questions and listening effectively to the answers is that it can provide you with some really valuable information. The more relevant information you can

"Many salespeople will ask initial questions, but they will often fail to keep probing once they receive the initial response"

extract from a prospect, the more chance you have of matching the features of your property to the requirements of their company. In other words, the more chance there is of achieving a sale. Unfortunately, while many salespeople will ask initial questions, they will often fail to keep probing once they receive the initial response.

Here's an example. You are in a conversation with the marketing director of a potential sponsor. It is your first meeting and you are trying to identify areas of interest:

"Mrs Newcombe, how helpful would it be to use this proposed sponsorship as the basis of a sales incentive programme?"

"Yes, that could possibly work." She responds.

"What about the chance to entertain clients?" And so you move on to find further areas of interest, thinking that you have gone as far as you need to at this stage.

What I would like to suggest is that you don't move on after the initial response to your question about sales incentives. Instead, I would probe a little deeper, to see if I can encourage the prospect to expand on their response and to be more explicit in explaining why this would be important:

"Yes, that could possibly work," she tells you.

"So how would you go about using the opportunity? You enquire.

"Well, I know our sales director is always trying to come up with innovative ideas for creating sales incentives for our sales team."

"Have any of these been based on a sponsorship programme in the past?"

"No, I don't think so"

"How successful have they been?"

"I believe that their effectiveness has tailed off over the last couple of programmes that he devised"

"How might the link to a company sponsorship help improve this?"

"Why don't you tell me?" she says, providing you with a great opportunity.

In the process, you have discovered something important. Although she apparently agreed that the opportunity to use the sponsorship as the basis for a sales incentive programme could be helpful, there was an underlying problem. By probing, you discovered that the sales director had a problem inasmuch as his incentive schemes obviously weren't working as well as they should. This has now given you the chance to demonstrate how your sponsorship opportunity could help change this situation.

Had you accepted her initial agreement, on face value, it may not have come to light until it was too late that she was only paying lip service to the potential effectiveness of sales incentive opportunities. By probing further than you might normally do, you will often find that a person's true feelings will come to the surface. This will not only help you to identify possible problem areas that you might have been unaware of, but it can often provide a real opportunity to gain a meaningful, not a token, commitment from your prospect. It's a tactic that I use a great deal. I find that by probing in this way, I am not only able to unearth a lot more information, but very often discover a person's real opinions.

You will have gathered by now, that I am a great believer in the power of questions and in the power of listening effectively. These are two of the most important skills that you can possess when you are sitting face-to-face with a prospective sponsor. However, there is another aspect of your sales meeting that I want to look at, which I feel can cause some problems if it isn't handled properly.

When we examined the various items that you can take with you into a meeting to support what you are presenting, I stressed that they should not be used as a crutch or in place of dialogue or discussion. Sales tools should be there to help you present your case, not to present it for you.

Knowing when to bring them into play is something that is very difficult to learn. It tends to come from experience. You might have spent £10,000 on a CD-Rom video presentation, but if you find that you are in a meaningful dialogue with your prospect, why break that off to bring out your laptop computer and run the programme? It could easily be counterproductive. If you genuinely feel that the best way to demonstrate a point, or to present your ideas, is to bring that into play, that's fine, but use your judgement on this very carefully.

The most likely sales tool that you will want to use is your sales presentation. Perhaps it's a PowerPoint programme, or maybe you want to use a flipchart style of presentation. Whatever you have decided to use, the way in which you bring it into play can make a big difference to the effectiveness of the presentation.

In my experience, I find that most salespeople use one of two methods. The first option is to run through it from A to Z, in the manner that many insurance and financial services salespeople who visit people in their homes, will do. Alternatively, you can make the presentation interactive, involving the other person as you move through it.

Personally, I prefer the latter style. The problem with the first method is that you are effectively telling the prospect to keep quiet while you do your thing! The last thing that I want at this stage is quiet prospects! I want them doing more talking than me.

I want to hear their thoughts, their opinions, their ideas and most of all I want their confirmation on the points that I am covering. It's only by getting them to talk to you that you will know whether you are heading in the right direction. Having said that, there is a huge difference between your prospect interacting with you as you move though the presentation, and the prospect taking over and interrupting everything that you are trying to say. You still need to be in control.

The way I like to handle this situation is by putting questions to the prospect as I move through the slides. We come back to the use of questions again. It is just as important at this stage, as it is in the dialogue that you have both before and after the presentation.

For example, when you get to the point in your presentation that deals with the range of possible entitlements, you might ask: "How helpful would it be to your sales force to be able to bring potential customers to our Formula 1 HQ to see the use of your software in our design office?"

Or: "How would you use the number of player personal-appearance days that you'd be entitled to?"

When you are going through the media coverage section, you might enquire: "Which section of the media is most important for your type of business?"

Or: "How important would regional TV coverage be to you?"

In this way, you not only keep control of the direction in which you want the presentation to go, but you also continue to build a picture of what is and what isn't important to your prospect. This will help you greatly when you come to putting together a tailored proposal.

Another aspect of the sales meeting that can cause a lot of problems is the question of money. In other words, that time in a conversation when the prospect asks the question "And how much is all this going to cost?"

"When the question of costs is posed, explain that you need to work out the specific cost based on the range of entitlements that he has agreed to"

If this subject hasn't been raised in your pre-meeting phone discussions, which I looked at earlier, you can bet your bottom dollar that it is going to come up in your first meeting with the potential sponsor. I think it is true to say that this is an area that worries a great number of people. You have a natural concern that the moment the prospect hears how much you want for your sponsorship opportunity, he or she will immediately drop it like the proverbial hot potato. It is very tempting to pre-judge this situation and by the time the question comes up, you have almost convinced yourself your fee is too high. If this is what you are thinking, it will almost certainly come out in the way that you reply to the question.

The first thing that you need to remember is that if you have done your homework correctly, as we saw early on in the book, your fee should already be set at the right level for the sponsorship opportunity you are presenting. Naturally, if you are going to subsequently present a personalised proposal, based on the specifically outlined requirements of your prospect, that value might rise or fall slightly, but you should still be fairly accurate. If this is the case, you needn't feel that you are asking too much for your sponsorship property and therefore should have the confidence to be up front about it. It's at this point that the true value of the preparation that I covered earlier becomes apparent. If you haven't done that preparation, you will have very little confidence in presenting a fee that is based purely on either guesswork, or the costs of the project.

Assume that you are in your first meeting with a company. Your objective is to leave with enough information so that you can then prepare a detailed proposal, based on the identified requirements of the prospect. By arranging to present this at a follow up meeting you will have gained the commitment that I stressed is so critical.

When the question about costs is posed you can explain that you will need to work out the specific cost, based on the range of entitlements that he has agreed are important to him. You will include this in the tailored presentation that you are going to be presenting at the next meeting. It is a reasonable comment to make.

However, he might persist and want an idea of what the final cost could be. If this is the case, you need to give him an indication. You should be able to provide a "between X and Y" response, which is reasonably accurate. You can add that it will depend very much on the level of sponsorship that is considered appropriate. If you try too hard to avoid answering his questions on fee levels, you will

Jean Alesi demonstrates the ever-changing world of sponsorship.
Above: His Jordan carries the soon-to-be-outlawed Benson & Hedges livery.
Left: With the Benetton F1 car at the sponsorship launch that Brian personally secured for both FedEx and Gillette.

create a degree of annoyance and risk losing the person's interest. They will begin to think that you have something to hide. You don't, providing that you have done your homework properly.

When you've given him the figures, it is important to get confirmation from him that this is a realistic expectation. In other words, you want to avoid the situation where as soon as you leave the room, he tears up your proposal and throws in it in the bin. You might have been asking for £150,000. He realised that his budget would only stretch to £50,000 and so he decided that he wouldn't waste any more time on the matter.

If this is a genuine concern of his, it is better to find this out while you are sitting in front of him and can possibly do something to resolve the problem. It could be, for example, that although this company cannot afford to be a primary sponsor, there could be an alternative option of being a lesser-status sponsor. This might involve designing a proposal that offers them a limited range of entitlements, but includes those main points that were seen as being very beneficial.

Another route that I have taken in this situation involves initially gaining the assurance from the prospect that it is only the price that is the problem. You need him to confirm that he likes the concept and the actual proposals, but that his marketing budget will not accommodate it. You need to be very sure at this stage that he's not trying it on, to be able to pay for the opportunity at a knockdown price. If you feel he is being genuine, why not suggest that one option for him is to perhaps invite some of his company's suppliers to take part as co-sponsors of the programme. This can work very well in practice. Maybe you could propose that he helps you secure some other co-sponsors, by introducing you to some of his business associates.

"You will have to haggle, but provided you know the true value of your property and how you arrived at that value, you are in a very strong position"

If you ascertain that what the prospect is telling you is that he wants to find a way of making the deal happen, you can usually come to an agreement that suits both parties.

When I first started putting together sponsorship deals, I was excited if I secured any figure above £500. Later on in my career, I put together deals in Formula 1 that involved many millions of pounds. The strange thing is that when I was sitting in the head office of a company like Marconi, Gillette or FedEx, the way in which the fee was discussed in millions of pounds bore little difference to the way that I discussed those very early deals that were in the hundreds. It's all relative. What might seem like a small fortune to you, sitting presenting a sponsorship proposal to a company, may be small fry to them. I know it is easy to say, but try to remember this when you are presenting your fee structure. Don't let the prospect see that you are nervous or unsure of yourself. You need to put across the impression that it is the most normal thing in the world to be informing him that the sponsorship opportunity will cost £350,000. Don't sound apologetic when you put it forward.

If you get the response that it is too expensive, you need to be absolutely sure as to whether your prospect means that the programme fee is out of his budget levels, or that he might be able to afford it, but thinks it is too expensive for what is being provided. It's vital that you know this. You will need to handle the objection carefully. I sometimes ask a question, such as: "Is it only the cost that is preventing you from moving forward?"

Or: "Can I clarify what you are saying? Is it the fact that it is over your budget limit or do you feel it doesn't warrant that fee?"

If you can get confirmation that the programme you are offering is of interest, but it is the cost that is the issue, you are probably entering the negotiation stage of the meeting. It's important to recognise this. What it really means is that you don't need to defend what you are offering. Instead, you need to start negotiating between what you are prepared to accept and what he is prepared to offer. You've probably done this on holiday in the market place, or in a bazaar, when you have been trying to buy something .You will have to haggle, but provided you know the true value of your property and how you arrived at that value, you are in a very strong position.

Ideally, you should show that what you are offering is not negotiable. Try to get the full price by going over all of the benefits that the prospect has agreed can be accrued. Unfortunately, however, in such a highly competitive environment, the reality is that the chances of getting exactly what you want are quite slim. It may be a good idea to identify a couple of areas that aren't really vital to the prospect and eliminate them from the proposal, dropping the price slightly to reflect this.

Personally, I always try to go about it from the other direction, which is to throw in some extra entitlements that will cost very little in reality. For example, an extra player-appearance day, or possibly some extra tickets to your event. In this way, you still keep the revenue level high and, although you've given something extra away, there is probably not a major direct cost to this.

In the event of the sponsorship fee being a problem, there is another strategy that you can introduce if you've done your homework on the subject carefully. It's known as performance bonus payments.

In Formula 1, it is quite common for a sponsorship fee to include performance bonus payments. What this means is that an agreement is reached with a sponsor where they will pay a percentage of the fee asked, perhaps 75 per cent. This will be a guaranteed payment to you. The balance will only be paid if you achieve certain performance related targets. Normally each specific target is linked to a fee that is payable on its achievement. This can provide a worthwhile opportunity for you to not only achieve you sponsorship fee target, but to also, in some cases, exceed it. The only proviso is that you must have confidence that the levels of performance can be achieved, or are attainable. For their part, companies wanting to consider this method of payment can take out specialist insurance to cover the eventuality.

Here is an example of the way in which performance bonus payments can work in association with a sponsorship agreement:

Suppose you are seeking £100,000 as a sponsorship fee for your powerboat team to compete in a national championship, comprising ten rounds. The sponsor has offered to pay a fee of just £75,000 for the proposed sponsorship package. What do you do?

A compromise might be to suggest that, in addition to the £75,000 fee, you agree on a bonus scheme, which can usually be covered by insurance. It might be structured as follows:

- For each victory in the championship — bonus payment of £5,000
- For each second or third place podium position — bonus payment of £1,500
- For first place overall in the championship — bonus payment of £15,000
- For second place overall in the championship — bonus payment of £7,500
- For third place overall in the championship — bonus payment of £5,000

In this way, it is conceivable that you could earn £65,000, in addition to the £75,000 sponsorship fee, by winning the championship and every race. Even if you won three races, and secured four third places, finishing outside of the top three in the championship, you would earn £21,000 in addition to the £75,000.

Perhaps you are a cricketer. A personal sponsorship programme might include a payment every time you hit a half-century, or take five wickets in a match. There are many ways in which you can structure an attractive performance bonus scheme that works for you and for the sponsor.

Multi-dimensional selling

It may well be that your initial proposal was designed to offer a multi-dimensional method of selling, of the type that we looked at in some detail. If it did, you would have discovered by this stage whether it is feasible and of interest. However, if you didn't, but have now identified such an opportunity, it is still not too late to incorporate this. You need to be very alert to an opportunity for presenting this type of strategy. It will depend very much on the feedback that you have received from your line of questioning. If you begin to sense that such an opportunity is opening up, it might be worth keeping it up your sleeve at this point of time. By all means put out a few more feelers to test the potential, but better to wait until you are able to incorporate it into the tailored presentation that you will submit at the follow-up meeting.

At the follow-up meeting you can add a surprise element, which will demonstrate a possible route by which the sponsor will be able to generate additional, measurable business as a result of your sponsorship proposals. This will be even more impressive than trying to explain this at the end of that first meeting.

Measurement of sponsorship performance

If you can build into your sponsorship proposals a measurement of performance against agreed objectives, I can promise you that you will be head and shoulders above most sponsorship-seekers.

What do I mean by measurement? Anything that will help the sponsor answer two very important questions:

1. "Am I getting value for money?"
2. "How do I know that the sponsorship is working for me?"

Measurement of sponsorship performance is a highly controversial subject. Opinions vary enormously on effective techniques of sponsorship measurement. As I mentioned in my opening chapters, there are specialist companies that are able to provide levels of measurement for a sponsor. The problem is that at the present time, there is no universal standard of measurement in place.

"By measuring the time a brand name appears in an event, a comparison can be made with other methods of achieving similar coverage"

Lots of supposed experts in the subject will have their own views on the matter, but what is needed is a method that is accepted by everyone involved in sponsorship, as to the accepted way of measuring achievement. Whether this will happen in the near future is very much open to debate.

The big problem is that sponsorship performance is not always simple to measure in strict, easily quantifiable terms. It is easier, for example, to measure the impact of a sponsorship that is based on the amount of brand awareness achieved in specified media sources. By measuring the number of seconds that a brand name appears in an event, a comparison can be made with other methods of achieving similar coverage.

On the other hand, measuring a sponsorship that is based on image transfer is far more difficult.

It could be argued that the measurement of hospitality effectiveness should be based upon the amount of business that is derived from guests – perhaps measured over the six months following their participation in the event. But how can that be accurate? For a start, you will never know whether or not that level of business might have come in anyway, without the expense of the sponsorship and hospitality.

You might be able to generate a business relationship between two sponsors of your team. You can then show that as a result of meeting up through the sponsorship activities they did X-pounds of business with each other. In other words, that success is measurable. Sales incentive programmes based on the sponsorship can provide a good form of measurement. It might be possible to show that sales during the incentive period were up by an above average amount. Again, this is a form of sponsorship measurement. PR is another area in which measurement guidelines can be introduced. The number of column inches of editorial coverage that were achieved by your sponsorship property will provide a measurement tool for you. This can be compared against the targeted amount.

The striking livery of the Benetton Formula One car after Brian sucessfully secured the deal for FedEx.

The most important thing to remember is to show your prospective sponsor that it is not your intention to take the money and not worry about delivering results. The very fact that you are prepared to raise the subject of measurement of performance against the sponsor's objectives, will add to the sponsor's respect for you.

If you are able to afford it, it can be very effective to retain the services of a sponsorship evaluation agency to measure the performance of the sponsorship. It shows your sponsor that you want this agreement to work for them, for a start. By offering to pay for the provision of this service you are also showing confidence in the property's ability to deliver what you are promising.

Even if you can't afford to do this, don't be afraid of suggesting to your sponsor that they might like to consider doing so for themselves. This is quite a normal practice.

If, on the other hand, you feel that this might show that the sponsor is not getting value for money, you really should not be approaching them in the first place.

Closing the meeting

There will be a point in the meeting when you realise that it is time to wind up. Perhaps the prospect is starting to look at his or her watch, or they might have indicated to their secretary that the meeting will be over in a few minutes time.

Be aware of these signs and don't overstay your welcome. That doesn't mean that you get up and walk out straight away. It's better to indicate to the prospect that you are aware of his or her time constraints and wait for a reaction. You may be told that you can have another few minutes, or it may be that you are asked to wind up.

What is important at this stage is to move into a summarising mode and then gain a commitment, in line with your objective. I don't mean that you simply run through every major part of the proposals that you have made during the meeting. What I normally do is to simply highlight the main points that I feel are significant, confirming as I run through these, the prospect's previous agreement that they were important. Here's an example:

"We looked at the opportunity that this programme offers your company, to develop a powerful and innovative sales incentive scheme, based on the calendar of events. You mentioned to me that you were looking for a new format and this could provide the answer. You also pointed out that this programme could provide your company with an excellent opportunity to develop a relationship with the local community. Finally, the opportunity to use some of the players for your company golf days would, as you agreed, add greater value to them."

When you have done this, it is vital that you gain a commitment towards the next step in the process. There are many ways of doing this and it will depend on what you want to achieve as to what these can be. Perhaps, for example, you want to invite the prospect and their colleagues to an event in which you are competing. Alternatively, you might want to diarise a meeting at which you will present a more detailed and tailored proposal, based on your findings in this meeting. Whatever it is, make sure you get this commitment.

"So having agreed that there is the basis of a workable sponsorship programme that meets you marketing requirements, would it make sense to invite you and your CEO to come to our next home match to sample some of the hospitality facilities and meet some of our directors?

Or: "Having agreed that this sponsorship programme can offer you all the points that we've just covered, what's the next step from your point of view?"

At which point you shut up and don't say anything more until he has answered.

SUMMARY

Listening is a rare quality amongst most salespeople. To listen properly, you shouldn't be thinking of your next response. Only by listening carefully and asking another question based on that reply will you uncover the real reasons for a prospect's opinions and reactions.

You will be surprised at the reaction of people to you if you are prepared to listen carefully to what they are saying. You will go up in their estimation quite considerably because it doesn't happen too often.

The way you use your sales presentation in a meeting can be very influential. You don't want to lose control of the meeting, but equally, you don't want to stop the prospect from asking questions or making observations. The way you effect the middle path is by the careful use of questions that encourage the prospect to confirm those points that he sees as being beneficial.

At some stage you are going to be asked about the fee that is involved. It is better to be up front about discussing this than to keep trying to avoid the matter.

If you genuinely haven't worked out a fee, because you need to put together a tailored proposal, then be open with the prospect and explain this. If the prospect persists in wanting a ballpark figure, you should provide a likely top and bottom of the range fee, so that you are not seen to be avoiding the issue.

When you have done this, you need to find out whether those two levels are both within his budget range. This will avoid wasting his and your time. If the price is raised as an objection, you need to find out whether it is because it is actually outside the prospect's budget or whether they feel that it is just too high for what is being offered.

By introducing a performance bonus scheme, you can sometimes solve the problem of the fee being too high in the prospect's opinion. If you can introduce a system that will help the prospect measure the effectiveness of the sponsorship, you will stand head and shoulders above the majority of sponsorship seekers.

NORW
UNI

PEREIRA

Gaining a **commitment**

I have usually found that if you achieve a second meeting, there is more than an even chance that your prospect is looking for a reason to enter into an agreement with you. It may not be the precise deal that you wanted, but for the sales process to continue in that way, there has to be a reasonable level of interest.

The ideal scenario is to gain a commitment for a second meeting while you are still in the first. It may be that you gained agreement to have a follow-up meeting at which you would submit a personalised and more detailed proposal, based on everything that was agreed in that initial discussion. Whatever the commitment you obtained, I cannot over-emphasise the importance of maintaining communication with the prospect beyond the first meeting.

To design and produce such a tailored presentation should be a great deal easier than the original. If you went about that meeting in the right way, you will have come away with a list of all the points that need to be included. This proposal will eventually form the basis of an agreement between you and the sponsor, so it is important to include everything that your prospect agreed would be beneficial. If you want to include your multi-dimensional plan, as we discussed at the end of the last chapter, you should do so now, but be careful not to contradict anything that has already been agreed, otherwise you might have to go back to square one and gain his commitment all over again.

It's always my aim to arrive at a situation in which the prospect feels that he is developing the sponsorship programme himself. As you have seen, I do this by the careful and planned use of questions, encouraging him to agree on the areas that would work well and discarding those that wouldn't. It is not so easy for him to then turn down a tailored proposal that has been structured around all of the points that he agreed were important and beneficial.

The time for the follow-up meeting has arrived. You should be a lot more relaxed for this meeting than you were at the first. You know that there is a level of interest and you have met the prospect before. However, it is still important to prepare as well for it as for the previous meeting. It's always a good idea to take with you some spare copies of the presentation or proposal, as there may be more than one person present at the meeting. You should also set yourself an objective. Ideally, this should be to obtain a positive decision in principle, before you leave the meeting. However, this will often depend very much upon the size of the company in question. If you are presenting to a large multi-national corporation, for example, it could be quite a long decision process and not possible to achieve in one more meeting. The FedEx deal I put together took me a total of four months and about twelve meetings in total. On the other hand, with a privately owned company you might even get a firm decision there and then. The higher up the company pecking order your prospect is, the faster a decision is normally taken.

Even if you don't get a decision in principle at this second meeting, it's important to get some form of commitment. It might be a further meeting, or it might be that you will provide some additional detailed information endorsing TV viewing figures. In one case, I had to prepare an internal proposal for the directors, which they in turn would send to their American bosses at the company's global HQ for approval.

I usually find that the second meeting is very different from the first and normally moves along quite well on its own, although it is still important to control it, as you hopefully did in the first one. As I said before, you wouldn't be there if there wasn't a reasonable level of interest within the company. What you need to do is to maintain your level of enthusiasm and a healthy dialogue, so that it reaches a successful conclusion.

"Another way of closing is to get a response on a relatively minor point of detail, which will effectively show agreement overall"

You should be at the stage by now where opportunities to close the deal start appearing. This is an area that has already been much written about by others. "Closing the sale", as it called, is a part of the sales process that is perhaps the most difficult. My suggestion is that you read some of the many books on selling that today fill the shelves of the bookshops. These will provide you with a range of methods that different sales exponents use. As I keep saying, there is no right or wrong way. It's what works best for you that matters.

All salespeople have their own way of going about the task. Some like to simply ask a direct question when they feel that the time is appropriate, such as: "So Mr Davies, having agreed that the opportunity presents so many beneficial entitlements for you, are you happy that we go ahead with the agreement?"

Another way of closing is to get a response on a relatively minor point of detail, which will effectively show agreement overall. This can often help a prospect reach a decision without too much heartache. Remember, you might be nervous at this stage, but so might your prospect. If the sponsorship goes wrong, he could be in trouble. Instead of asking him the big question, "Do you want to go ahead?" ask him a question that is more concerned with a point of detail.

"Where would you like to hold the launch party?"

"Which of the two colour schemes are you going to adopt?"

"Which stage payment schedule suits you the best?"

I should stress yet again that at this stage you now keep quiet and wait for the prospect to answer. By responding to these questions, the prospect is effectively agreeing to the proposal without facing the "Yes" or "No" situation that a direct question would necessitate.

Another option is to use a question that provides the prospect with two alternatives, neither of which is to respond with a negative:

"Would you prefer to start the agreement on the September 1st, or would you rather have it commence in your new financial year?"

"Which of the two options makes the most sense for you, the title sponsorship or the co-sponsorship programme?"

It is quite normal to have to attempt your closing process several times. However, it is better to do this than to leave the meeting without trying one close. In selling, asking for the order is something that a lot of people find very difficult. It comes back to the point that I raised right at the beginning of the book. One of the problems that people identify with selling is the fear of rejection. You perhaps worry that if you try to close the deal you'll get a firm "No". You might feel that if you keep the discussion going, you won't get a rejection.

The thing about closing is that it will tell you whether you are heading in the right direction. If you have made a good job of gaining commitment all along the route, a positive close should come almost naturally to the process. If you find, however, that the prospect raises an objection, the nature of that will indicate whether you are near to a positive close, or whether you need to go back to your questioning process and uncover the underlying problem area.

If you have been successful in obtaining a positive response to your close, you need to confirm the fact as quickly as possible, ideally by means of a document called a "letter of intent". I'll explain what this is shortly.

It is quite likely, at this stage, that you might not be able to secure a response, either negative or positive. On many occasions, you'll be told that the prospect intends to discuss matters with his colleagues and then get back to you. Some salespeople might try to push the point and ask what he needs to discuss. It's my experience that if you are not careful, you can irritate people in this way. What is being suggested is normal practice. What I will usually do is to ask the prospect if there are any particular points that he would like me to clarify further before he does this. I will also normally ask if it would it be helpful for me to be at that meeting. If the answer is "No thank you", I don't push my luck any further.

Once you get to this stage of the sales process, it becomes very much more difficult to help you. If you haven't reached a specific conclusion in the meeting, but have been asked to wait for a response, one of two things will usually happen:

1. You receive a letter or phone call that informs you that, after careful consideration, the company has decided not to move forward. You then have to make a decision. Do you accept this negative response and plan a different way of attacking the issue? Or, do you decide to cut your losses and move on to the next prospect? This is very much up to you and will depend on how many other companies you are talking to at the time. It will also depend on what you believe the reason to be and whether you can come up with an acceptable solution. If you feel that you can, then you should go for it, but be careful not to waste a lot more time unless you genuinely think you can turn it around.
2. You get a positive response from your contact. This might mean that a decision has been made to accept your proposal. More often, it will mean being told that that the company wants to continue with further discussions. In this case, I normally find that the sales process starts to gather a momentum of its own. The way in which it does this will, to a certain extent, be dictated by the actions and requirements of your prospect.

You might be asked to present your ideas to the board of the company at yet another meeting, or it could be that the prospect wants to involve the CEO and financial director for an informal discussion on the plan's implementation. Very often, it can be that the company wants to go ahead with the proposals, but tells you that the fee is too high. This will mean you are entering the negotiation phase of the sales process.

The art of successful negotiation is a complex subject, which requires a book on its own, but much of it will be down to common sense. The higher the fee you are demanding, the more negotiation there will be. If you are very inexperienced as to how to go about this, and you are talking about a sponsorship fee in excess of £100,000, I would strongly recommend you bring in a lawyer or even your accountant to help in the process. A show of strength doesn't do any harm, as long as you decide with this accompanying person in advance what your limits of negotiation are.

"A Letter of Intent isn't a legally-binding document, but it will be a major step in the process of securing a signed agreement"

Once you have reached this stage in the sales process, you will need to consider how you will go about finally closing the sale and getting a commitment in writing. This is important, because life has a horrible knack of throwing up some unpleasant surprises. Imagine if your contact suddenly decides to leave the company, or is knocked over by a bus. If you have nothing in writing, there is a strong chance that the sponsorship might be postponed or, even worse, cancelled. It's very important to not only gain approval for your proposals, but to get that approval in writing as soon as possible.

The easiest way of doing this is to prepare and have with you a "Letter of Intent". While this isn't a legally-binding document, it will be a major step in the process of securing a signed agreement and will give you more protection than a verbal assurance. It is well worth asking your solicitor to draft such a document. Hopefully, this example will give you an idea of what is required:

Letter of intent
This is a Letter of Intent between (Sponsor) Highlands Flight Services Company of 37/45 Ayr Road, Dundee, Scotland:

(You) Jetline Racing Ltd of Unit 7, Park Industrial Estate, Northampton, Northants, dated this (current date) 3rd day of September 2004

Dear "Mr Smith of Jetline Racing",
Following meetings on the 23rd April and 4th July, 2004, at which proposals were put forward by Jetline Racing to Highland Flight Services concerning possible sponsorship of the team in the 2005 National Powerboat Championship, it is hereby confirmed that Highland Flight Services intends to accept these proposals and enter into a three-year sponsorship agreement with Jetline Racing.

This acceptance is conditional upon the terms and conditions of any subsequent legally binding contract being acceptable to the Directors of Highland Flight Services.

It is understood that the agreement will be based on the points outlined in the attached document and contained in the proposal dated 29th July. (Attach a copy of the proposal)

I look forward to receiving a draft copy of the contract from your lawyer in due course.

Yours sincerely,
On behalf of Highland Flight Services.

Kelly Holmes' success at the 2004 Olympics can't be guaranteed with every athlete or sports team, but honesty about their prospects can greatly enhance the relationship between you and the sponsor

This is a normal business practice. Although it isn't in itself legally binding, it will speed up the eventual process of having the contract drafted by your lawyer and should provide you with some peace of mind. Such a letter will confirm in writing the main points on which the subsequent legal agreement will be based. As a guideline, it will include the entitlements that the sponsor will receive and the fees that he will pay for these entitlements. It will not include all the normal legal information about termination, breach of contract and so on. This will only appear in the legal document. The Letter of Intent will make it much easier for the two sets of lawyers to reach an agreement and will help to keep your costs down.

It's well worth mentioning the length of duration of an agreement. It is always best to push hard for a long-term agreement with a sponsor. By this I mean typically a three-year deal. The reason for this is that it genuinely benefits both parties.

For a sponsor, there can be a problem with a one-year agreement. It can be argued that the first year of a sponsorship is very often the most expensive. This might be because of the one-off costs involved in branding vehicles or producing promotional and advertising materials. To recoup the full value of this will not be so easy if it is going to be measured over a single year. It's true to say that most sponsorships only become really effective in their second and third years. Unless there is a high level of previous experience, it often takes a sponsor the best part of the first year to tune the programme to gain maximum impact.

From your point of view, a long relationship will give you the chance to prove to the sponsor just what you are capable of delivering on their behalf. It will also relieve some of the pressure that you are bound to feel, knowing that halfway through the agreement you will need to start looking at a possible renewal.

Once you have obtained a signed Letter of Intent, the next step is to ask your legal representative to draft a formal and legally binding agreement, based on the contents of the proposal that has been accepted. My advice on this, unless you already have a lawyer who understands the subject, is to go to one of the many lawyers that now specialise in sports sponsorship contracts. You can obtain the names of those in your area by contacting the Law Society and asking for their help. It will save you a great deal of hassle, because he or she will know just what should go into the agreement, unlike a lawyer looking at this for the first time. It will also save you money in the long run. Some lawyers will have standard agreements already prepared which can be personalised to your particular deal.

You might feel that if the sponsorship is only very small, it's not worth the trouble and expense of having a formal contract drawn up. That is obviously for you to decide. My experience of contracts is that they are usually put into the drawer, forgotten about and the only time they are looked at is when something goes wrong. It's at that point that you need one.

It is the case with most sponsorship agreements that the sponsor will insist on a legally drawn up contract. Although this can involve you in some expense, it does give both parties full protection. The more complex the deal that you have agreed, the more reason there is to have a formal agreement. Similarly, the higher the fee, the more essential the need for a legal agreement becomes.

"When it comes to negotiating, you should ideally try to add extra entitlements that do not have a real cost to you, and keep the fee at the same level"

Sometimes your sponsor will insist that his lawyers prepare the sponsorship agreement themselves. This is often the case with a company that is an experienced sports sponsor. I wouldn't be too concerned about this, provided that you still use your own lawyer to check it through. It might even save you some money.

The last point, but most certainly not the least important, is that before you sign a sponsorship agreement, you must be 100 per cent certain that you will be able to deliver everything that you are committing to. If you're not sure, don't sign it until you've sorted it out. It's no good signing the agreement and, when a thorny issue is raised, saying that you didn't fully understand it. Neither is it any use assuming that if you can't deliver entitlements to the absolute letter of the contract, a company won't really mind. It's my experience that they normally do mind. They mind very much!

SUMMARY

If you are able to secure a second meeting, the likelihood is that your prospect has a genuine interest in trying to reach a successful conclusion. It is quite likely that you will use this second meeting to present a tailored sponsorship proposal which is based on all the points that the prospect agreed were important at that first meeting.

It will almost certainly form the basis for your eventual sponsorship agreement, so make sure that you include as many entitlements as you feel necessary, but try to keep some up your sleeve as a negotiating tool. When it comes to negotiating, you should ideally try to add extra entitlements that do not have a real cost to you, and keep the fee at the same level rather than exclude entitlements and have to reduce the price.

At the second meeting, you should be thinking about gaining a commitment. A Letter of Intent can prove very helpful in this respect. It pays to go for a three-year agreement or, at worst, a two-year period. Both parties will benefit from this.

The Letter of Intent is not legally binding, but is the precursor to a full sponsorship agreement. It lists what both parties have agreed will be the basis on which the sponsorship deal is to be structured. It is worth involving a lawyer in the process of drafting the actual sponsorship agreement. You should try to find a specialist in sports sponsorship, as this will save you time and therefore, money.

Never enter into a sponsorship agreement unless you are confident that you can deliver all of the entitlements that you have agreed.

Is there **intent?**

W hen I started out in my motor racing career, I was no different to many other drivers in wanting to climb the ladder to the very pinnacle of the sport, Formula 1.

I realised early on that it wasn't going to happen as a driver, for two reasons:

1. I had started too late, at the age of 28.
2. I wasn't determined enough to give up everything else in life.

By recognising this, I was able to capitalise on the skills that I did possess and build a career, which eventually led me to Formula 1, but not as a driver. I remember the excitement that I felt when I secured my first-ever Formula 1 sponsorship deal with Gillette, on behalf of the Benetton F1 Team. Although there is nothing that compares with the adrenalin rush that you experience at the start of a race, the phone call that I received from Gillette, informing me that the deal was going ahead, came pretty close.

My most satisfying deal was undoubtedly the FedEx sponsorship, also on behalf of Benetton. To start a process, literally with a cold call, and then to work your way through four months of meetings, presentations and negotiations in Europe, the UK and America is quite an exhausting process. However, when the two F1 cars, driven by Jean Alesi and Alex Wurz, appeared with FedEx branding at the British Grand Prix at Silverstone, it all became worthwhile.

It wasn't always plain sailing with Benetton, however. The Company was renowned at that time for its highly controversial global poster campaign. It cost me a potential sponsorship deal.

I had made contact with Guerlain, the French perfumery company, to discuss sponsorship opportunities. My proposals were well received initially, as Benetton F1 fitted well with a female product range and it was quite common for United Colours of Benetton to arrange fashion shoots around its F1 cars at a Grand Prix. However, when the time came for me to present to the Guerlain marketing director, there was a distinct change of attitude. I was informed that that the company was about to launch a new perfume called Champs-Elysées. Its image was typified in the advertising by virginal young ladies tripping through the daisy-filled meadows, under a sunny sky, with the birds singing. The packaging was going to be all pink. She then went on to tell me that, in her opinion, Benetton's latest poster campaign, that showed a black stallion mounting a white mare in a field, didn't quite fit with the image that they were seeking!

In the process of writing this book, I've remembered a lot of things that, over the years, I'd almost forgotten about professional selling. As I'm still busy consulting on sports sponsorship for various clients, it's been a great help to me, reminding me of some of the basics that tend to get forgotten. It has also endorsed my belief that, however much experience you may have and however successful you may have been, in this business you never stop learning.

In the last chapter, we reached the stage of the sales process where you should be leaving the prospect's office with a signed Letter of Intent clutched firmly in your hand. As a result, I have almost achieved what I set out to do when I decided to write the book. My objective was to help you increase your chances of securing sports sponsorship. Right at the start, I emphasised that I can only provide you with a guide to the sponsorship selling process. I can't hold your hand and take you through every step because each meeting will be different and every person you meet will have their own way of progressing matters with you. It's rather like learning to drive. I can teach you the basics and give you a good grounding in the subject, but only experience will turn you into a good driver. Despite having been in this business a long time, I still read as many books as I can on selling techniques and practices. I would recommend that you do the same, if you are serious about improving your performance when you are face-to-face with your prospect.

"If you have done your job properly, the sponsor will come to trust and rely on you to help make a programme even more successful as it develops"

If this book does nothing more than provide you with a platform on which you can build and develop your skills to a much higher level, then I will consider my efforts worthwhile.

I said that I had almost achieved what I set out to do when I started this book. Almost – but not quite! What I haven't yet done is to highlight one of the most important aspects of the sponsorship process. How do you keep your sponsor on board? Although this book is primarily aimed at helping you to secure new sponsors, I can't complete it without a brief look at this important topic.

Finding new sponsors is one of the most difficult of all sales activities. The task is getting tougher by the day as more and more individuals, teams, clubs, associations and organisations enter the market, all wanting their slice of the sponsorship cake.

It doesn't need a rocket scientist to work out that it's far more cost-effective to look after the sponsors that you have already managed to secure than it is to keep looking for new ones. By developing a long-term relationship with your sponsor, you will both benefit greatly. You will learn just what is important to the sponsor and should therefore be able to modify your programme to suit their specific requirements. The sponsor will increasingly come to understand the sport and how it can be exploited to provide it with a commercial return. If you have done your job properly, the sponsor will come to trust and rely on you to help make the programme even more successful as it develops.

If you work hard at developing a good two-way communication with an existing sponsor, there is every reason to believe that you can increase the scope and size of the agreement that you initially negotiated. Very often, long-term major sponsorship programmes have resulted from a small initial involvement. It's not unreasonable to expect a company entering the world of sports sponsorship for the first time, to be rather reluctant to commit to a big spend until it has fully understood what sponsorship is all about. You need to take responsibility for helping its personnel realise the full potential of the sponsorship. If you can show them what can be achieved by

Gerhard Berger won the German Grand Prix at Hockenheim – despite Brian's caution to new sponsors, FedEx, not to expect much from the first season

expanding their involvement, you may well end up with a long-term major sponsor way beyond your initial expectation.

The key to sponsorship development is to make sure that you deliver more than your sponsor expects, not less. It's all too easy to be fired up and enthusiastic in the early days of a sponsorship, when everyone is excited about the prospects that lie ahead. It's when you are midway through the season that it can become more difficult to maintain this early enthusiasm. Perhaps results haven't gone your way. Maybe a couple of events have been rained off. It could be that you've realised that you are spending more than you budgeted for and on top of all that, you're beginning to get fed up with the sponsor's increasing demands. This is the testing time in the relationship. It can easily go belly-up from this point on and all that is left is for both parties to finish off the season as quickly as possible and part company. On the other hand, it can be the turning point in strengthening the association and building a solid foundation on which a long-term relationship can be developed. It is very much up to you as to which route you take.

One of the most common complaints from sponsors is the lack of communication from the sponsored party. During the build-up to the agreement being signed, they have received a string of phone calls and occasional visits checking that everything is still okay. Now that the first stage payment has been made, the communication suddenly dries up. Occasionally, a press release finds its way onto the sponsor's desk, but that's all that is heard from the sponsored party. Is it surprising that the sponsor starts to become somewhat concerned and even annoyed?

One way that I used to ensure that this didn't happen was to instigate a procedure aimed at maintaining communication. I did this right at the commencement of the sponsorship. It involved recommending to the sponsor the establishment of a small working group within the company, to be given the day-to-day responsibility of managing the sponsorship. Depending on the size of the company, this might include a representative from financial control. I would then have regular meetings throughout the period of the sponsorship with this group. In this way, we built up a relationship that was capable of working through difficult and good times together, with a level of understanding of each other's requirements.

The decision-maker with whom I had negotiated the deal rarely took part in this group, but appointed someone suitable to represent him. By having this regular meeting, I found that if there were any problems, they were not allowed to fester and become really serious. Instead, they would be spotted early on and action could be taken to manage the situation. It also provided me with the chance to make further proposals for ways in which the sponsor could get even more out of the arrangement. It's a method that I would strongly recommend to you.

"Something else that will help you to maintain a good relationship with your sponsor is known as the management of expectation"

It's important to avoid burying your head in the sand if there is a problem on the horizon. In my experience, problems seldom go away and have a habit of growing in importance the more you try to ignore them. Most people in management will understand that problems occur with any business, no matter how large or how efficient it might be considered. What they are more concerned about is the way that the problems are dealt with. It's the same as if you have ordered a meal in a restaurant and the meat hasn't been cooked in the way that you requested. Provided someone apologises and does their best to rectify the matter by bringing a perfectly cooked replacement meal, you will more than likely be satisfied. If they start arguing with you, or if the second meal is no better than the first, that's when most people start getting irritated.

It's the same with problems in sponsorship. As an example, if you learn that a particular round of a championship may be cancelled and you know that your sponsor is planning major hospitality at that event, don't leave it until the last minute to inform him of the imminent problem. You may hope that it will resolve itself, but very often it won't. Rather, approach the sponsor straight away and tell him about the situation as it currently stands. You should also try to develop a contingency plan, which you can suggest to him at the same time. If you only present the problem, without a possible solution, it won't be as well received as if you had given some thought to ways of dealing with the matter.

Something else that will help you to maintain a good relationship with your sponsor is what I always refer to as the "management of expectation". What this does is to ensure that the expectations of both parties going into a sponsorship agreement are on a similar level. A good example of this is to look at anticipated performance levels. You might fool a sponsor at the beginning of the relationship into believing that you are going to clean up in your championship. If you know that this isn't likely to be the case, you're doing yourself no favours. It can also work in reverse, however.

I recall that when I put the FedEx deal together, Benetton F1 was going through a very lean period, following the departure of Michael Schumacher. He had won the World Driver's Title in 1994 and 1995, in addition to the team winning the World Constructors' Championship in 1995. In my discussions with FedEx, I deliberately played down the level of expectation in terms of likely results for the 1997 season. Their sponsorship started midway through the season, at Silverstone.

The departure of Michael Schumacher from the Benetton team led to a new opportunity for sponsors to come on board and achieve a high profile for less outlay than they may have anticipated

Results up to that point had been very poor. However, to everyone's amazement, the team achieved a second and a third place in the British Grand Prix. We then went to Germany and Gerhard Berger, who had missed the previous three races, won the Grand Prix at Hockenheim. By now, the FedEx directors were asking me why I had been so pessimistic about potential results!

The next race was in Hungary and unfortunately the results went back to a more realistic level with an eighth and an eleventh place.

Controlling the level of expectation of a sponsor is a very important aspect of managing a sponsorship. If they expect too much, because of the build-up that you have given them, and the results don't match their expectations, it can prove an embarrassment for you. You need to work hard at creating the right balance.

Another important part of maintaining a good relationship with your sponsor is to ensure that the company's own staff is involved from the outset. It's worth talking to your new sponsor about this early on in your discussions. This applies equally to small companies as well as large corporations. I've seen several sponsorships die a death because of the internal politics that can arise from a lack of staff involvement in the new programme. I have often suggested to sponsors that they have a proper staff launch of the programme to tie in with the media launch. Let their own people understand why the company is involving itself in the sponsorship, so that they don't see it simply as a great expense, with little return.

Innovative staff-incentive programmes can be based on a sponsorship, with specials trips to events for staff and their families. Also, regular newsletters for internal readership are rarely a waste of time. It can also be a good idea to make yourself or perhaps your team's players, if applicable, available to visit staff functions, or maybe a charity event that the staff has organised, such as a sports day, a children's party or even a golf tournament. Even if it isn't written into your agreement, you should try to make that extra effort. It will pay dividends later when it comes to assessing and renewing the agreement. The more effort you put in, the greater the chance of the deal being renewed or expanded.

I've found that an existing sponsor appreciates nothing more, than your continual efforts help that company develop new business relationships. It pays to actively take an interest in the

"It's all about helping the sponsor achieve and surpass the objectives that you both set at the outset of the sponsorship"

business growth areas that they are targeting. Try to come up with some new ideas as to how they could use the sponsorship to help achieve introductions or meetings and you'll be well looked upon. Perhaps you could suggest that in your search for co-sponsors, you might approach some of the companies that they have identified as being on their own target list. In the process, you can suggest potential multi-dimensional alliances that might work for your existing sponsor and which could help them gain a foothold in the new business sector.

It's all about helping the sponsor achieve and surpass the objectives that you both set at the outset of the sponsorship. If you display a genuine interest in making sure that the sponsor gets every last ounce of value out of the agreement, you are far more likely to renew the deal.

For sponsorship to be successful, it has to be a two-way relationship. If it only works well for one of the two parties involved, it cannot be classed as being anything other than unfulfilled potential.

SUMMARY

Obtaining sponsorship is an extremely difficult task. Once you have secured a sponsor it makes sense to put a great deal of effort into keeping the company happy and eager to renew at the end of the initial sponsorship period.

One of the main complaints from sponsors is that the level of communication between the sponsored party and themselves declines rapidly once the deal has been signed.

It is worth structuring an effective communication channel, so that you can regularly meet with the key people who will be involved in monitoring and managing the sponsorship programme. At these meetings, you can advise them of opportunities that might arise and also of any imminent problems.

It is always better to draw any likely problems to the attention of the sponsor before they grow in importance. If you can, when you present the problem, try to present some possible solutions.

If you can develop a relationship with the sponsor in which you try to help them develop new business, using the sponsorship as the catalyst, you will be well looked upon.

It is important to convince the sponsor of the need to ensure that the majority of his staff buy into the sponsorship by involving them in activities and keeping them informed of progress within the sponsorship.

A solid **foundation**

We've covered a lot of ground together in this book. While I was considering what should be included in it, I spent a considerable amount of time trying to identify my likely target audience. Many of you who have read it may be experienced sponsorship seekers, flicking through its pages to see if there is some new approach that you can adapt for your own use. If that is the case, I hope you're not too disappointed in finding that there is little that is new in this tough business. Mostly it's a case of sticking to the basic principle of selling, which is to ascertain just what it is that your prospect is trying to achieve and then help them identify ways in which your sponsorship property can assist them in that task. Even the most experienced salespeople sometimes forget that simple philosophy.

There may be many of you who have read the book who will admit to being very inexperienced in the skills of sponsorship seeking. Some of you may even be parents of youngsters involved in various sporting activities. A number of these activities are now becoming so costly that they necessitate commercial sponsorship. It may be that lots of you have never had to look for sponsorship before and bought this book because you really had no idea where to start.

Hopefully there will be some readers who are just embarking on a career in sports marketing or in related areas. Perhaps you have gained a degree in a sports-related subject and you are seeking that all-important first job in the sports sector. I was astonished to learn that there are now over 1,500 degree courses at British universities, related to sport in some way. If you fall into this category, I really hope that you get as much enjoyment out of your future career as I have had during mine.

Whatever your level of experience, I hope that you have found this book to be both interesting and helpful. It's not an easy subject to write about because every situation you face will no doubt be very different. You are all individuals with varying skills, and desires. Unfortunately, there isn't a set format that will take you through a sales meeting, unless you have the ability to programme your prospect so that he or she asks the right questions at the correct time!

Training someone to sell is very different from training a plumber, or even an accountant, where there are specific right and wrong ways of handling most situations. In selling, there are few black and white areas; most are different shades of grey.

It is difficult to teach empathy, for example. Empathy is defined as the ability to sense the feelings of another person as though they were your own. It is a vital skill within the sponsorship sales process, but one that I believe only comes with experience. What you are in effect doing is putting yourself in the position of the other person, so that you can see things from their perspective. Few of us manage to do this in everyday life, let alone in a business meeting, however, if you make a genuine effort, I can promise you that it will make a huge difference to the way that you come across to your prospect.

Learning how to obtain sponsorship, whether for a one-off activity, or for a career in sports marketing, is very much about gaining experience. If you can put a strong foundation in place on which to build that experience, you will be far more successful. A good comparison is someone who wants to learn golf. Give that person a set of golf clubs and the use of a golf course and they might eventually find a way of achieving a not too embarrassing score. It's almost certain, however, that they will make a lot of mistakes and develop many bad habits along the way.

"If you have the enthusiasm, as well as the confidence that comes from thorough preparation, you can be as successful as anyone"

On the other hand, had they been given a course by a professional, showing them the basics of the game, they would undoubtedly have saved themselves a great deal of time and effort. More importantly, they would still have been able to develop their own style of golf in their own time. By knowing what they should be doing at any particular moment, they can gradually introduce their own style. They would be far less likely to develop any bad habits, which become more difficult to iron out the longer they are left.

That really sums up the purpose of this book. It is intended to provide you with the same solid foundation on which to build your own style of selling to prospective partners. It should help you identify your own strengths and weaknesses and work on them both to develop an individual, yet effective, style of your own.

I hope that you will decide to try out some of the ideas and suggestions that I've included, but please don't be too disappointed if they don't immediately bring about the results you want. It will take time to perfect the ways of delivering different strategies. You will also need to mould them to suit your own style of presentation.

At the end of this book, I have included four case studies, which I've selected to demonstrate some of the reasons why companies become sponsors. Although only one of these was a deal that I personally put together, I have chosen them because they are not multi-million pound Formula 1 deals. They are sponsorship programmes that have been entered into for sound business reasons, at a level that is affordable to most medium-sized companies. The principles that apply in these four studies can just as easily be applied to any sport at any level.

As I said right at the very beginning of the book, everyone can sell. Some people just find that it comes much easier to them than it does to others. If you decide that sponsorship is important to you, for whatever reason, you have two choices: you can either find someone to act on your behalf, or else you can decide to set about the task yourself.

I would like to think that after reading this book, you'll realise that if you have the enthusiasm, as well as the confidence that comes from thorough preparation, you can be as successful as anyone in the business. Go for it!

Chapter 22

Summary

1. You need to fully appreciate the number of reasons why companies use sports sponsorship as an important part of their marketing programmes. There are many more of these than most people realise. Although brand awareness and hospitality are perhaps the two most common uses of sponsorship, the more uses that you can identify within a company, the more successful you will be in matching your sponsorship property to its marketing requirements.

2. You need to create a sponsorship property that is saleable and priced at a realistic market level. You do this by identifying as many of the features that your property can deliver as possible. The more options that you have at your disposal, the more likelihood there will be that you can tailor a proposal that will fit the real, not assumed, needs of your prospective sponsor. You should be able to justify the fee level that you have placed on the property, by knowing that you arrived at that figure in a logical, calculated manner.

3. Use your creative powers and business acumen to devise an innovative sales strategy. One way of achieving this is to use the sponsorship property as a catalyst around which to build multi-dimensional business-to-business relationships.

Another effective way is to use the media as a powerful marketing tool and build strong media partnerships, which will help you attract commercial sponsors. The more effort and imagination that you can put into coming up with some really creative options at this stage, the easier you will find it to gain interest and secure meetings.

4. If you have put the effort into devising an innovative sales strategy, it will make the task of selecting which companies you are going to target a great deal easier.

When you start the process of selecting target companies, it's important to prepare a list of criteria that will help you narrow down your choice. It can prove very advantageous to target companies by business sector.

In this way, you will learn a great deal about the industry sector and just what is important to companies within it, from a marketing point of view. It will help you to identify the major players and who the companies are targeting for new business.

5. Research is a very important aspect of the sales process. If you approach the task in the right manner, you can find out a great deal of information that will help you build a picture of the company you are approaching – including its aims and objectives. It can, for instance, help you avoid possible minefields if you can discover a past sponsorship history. Research should indicate the decision-making hierarchy and help you understand the geographical operation of the company. Used effectively, it can even help you secure a meeting with the decision-maker at the appropriate stage of the sales process.

"You have worked hard to get the meeting and you don't want to waste the opportunity by not being prepared. You need to take the lead"

6. Having prepared a sales strategy and then, through research, pinpointed the companies you are going to contact, you can now design and create effective sales tools. This includes your sales presentation. Selling tools can be used to achieve your objective of securing a meeting as well as adding support to your sales dialogue in the meeting.

The sales presentation is the most important of all your sales tools. It needs to be flexible and easy to update. It should not be too wordy, but it is important that it is designed as a sales presentation, not simply as a showcase for past sports performances. It needs to demonstrate graphically how effective your property can be at providing the prospect's company with a cost-effective marketing platform.

Finally, sales tools should be used to support you, not replace you. It's important to know when to bring them into play and when to push them aside.

8. There comes a time when your planning and research has to stop and you need to make contact with the companies that you have targeted, for the purpose of securing a meeting. Whichever method you use, you need to be aware that your objective in making contact is only to secure a face-to-face meeting, not to try and sell the sponsorship in one go. It is important to find the method that works best for you and then focus on improving and fine-tuning it until it becomes really effective.

You need to use every ounce of initiative to find your way through the barriers that are increasingly being put in place in the corporate world to protect their marketing staff. This is where the research that you have carried out will stand you in good stead. You need to grab the attention of companies in a way that makes the right personnel want to find out more. It's a fine balancing act between giving them too much information, which will allow them to make a decision, or not enough to whet their appetite.

9. Once you have secured that first meeting, you need to prepare carefully and to be able to lead the meeting in the direction that you want to it to go. Don't go into a meeting and just hope that it will take the correct course. You have worked hard to get the meeting and you don't want to waste the opportunity by not being prepared. You need to take the lead from the first few moments. That doesn't mean you dominate the meeting by talking over the top of your prospect, it means that you set the tone by asking the right questions and listening to the answers, gradually steering the meeting in the direction that you want it to head.

It is important to obtain some form of commitment before you end the meeting. It might be that you set a date for a follow up meeting, or it could be that you arrange a meeting at your own premises to show the prospects the facilities available. Whatever you do, it is critical that you don't walk away without that commitment.

10. If you have done your job properly, you should have gained a firm commitment at the first meeting. Even if this involved setting a date and time for a second meeting, you will still need to follow up on that initial meeting. Apart from anything else, you need to either write to or email the person you had the meeting with and thank them for their time and interest. If a meeting has been arranged, then confirm this in the communication. If you left the meeting without any form of commitment, it's important for you to follow up directly with that person, to try to determine their reaction to your proposals. If you can make contact, you need to do everything that you can to get a commitment at this stage. If you don't, you are in danger of losing the momentum that you have built up. Remember, the commitment doesn't have to be for the deal itself, although that would be great. It needs to be a commitment as to the next step in the sales process.

"If you left the meeting without any form of commitment, it's important for you to follow up directly with that person"

11. You will eventually get a feel for the way the situation is progressing. When you believe that you are getting close to the decision stage, you should prepare a document that can be signed at the time of that decision. This should confirm the main points that you and the prospect have agreed will form the basis of the sponsorship contract. A "Letter of Intent", as it is called, is a valuable document, although it is not normally legally binding.

12. Having obtained your "Letter of Intent", signed by the prospect, you need to draft a legally binding agreement, ideally with the help of a professional solicitor who specialises in sports sponsorship agreements. This will then be submitted to the company, which will in turn almost certainly make some changes. Without the help of a legal representative at this stage, you might end up signing an agreement that isn't necessarily in your favour and I would stress that the money you spend, seeking professional advice, is money well spent.

13. Once you have achieved your objective of securing a commercial sponsor, you are only at the beginning of the workload. You need to make sure that you keep your new sponsor happy and help the company achieve the agreed objectives. The first step in this process is to maintain a regular method of communication and to identify in advance any problem areas that may arise. By dealing with these at the beginning, you will save yourself a great deal of trouble. If you allow them to fester, they could develop into a major altercation. It is far easier, and less expensive, to put in the effort to retain a sponsor than it is to keep searching for new ones.